COMPREHENSIVE RESEARCH
AND STUDY GUIDE

Robert
Browning

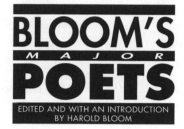

BLOOM'S
MAJOR
POETS

EDITED AND WITH AN INTRODUCTION
BY HAROLD BLOOM

COMPREHENSIVE RESEARCH
AND STUDY GUIDE

Robert Browning

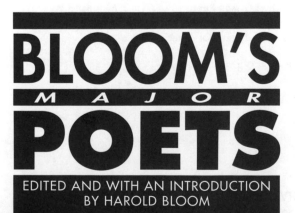

BLOOM'S *MAJOR* POETS

EDITED AND WITH AN INTRODUCTION
BY HAROLD BLOOM

Bloom's Major Poets: Robert Browning

Chelsea House
An imprint of Infobase Publishing
132 West 31st Street
New York NY 10001

Library of Congress Cataloging-in-Publication Data
Robert Browning / edited and with an introduction by Harold Bloom
        p. cm. — (Bloom's major poets)
    Includes bibliographical references and index.
    ISBN 0-7910-5931-6 (alk. paper)
    1. Browning, Robert, 1812–1889—Criticism and interpretation—
Handbooks, manuals, etc. 2. Browning, Robert, 1812–1889—
Examinations—Study guides. I. Bloom, Harold. II. Series.
PR4238.R58 2000
821'.8—dc21   00-055589

Chelsea House books are available at special discounts when purchased in bulk quantities for businesses, associations, institutions, or sales promotions. Please call our Special Sales Department in New York at (212) 967-8800 or (800) 322-8755.

You can find Chelsea House on the World Wide Web at
http://www.chelseahouse.com

Contributing Editor: Jesse Zuba
Produced by: Robert Gerson Publisher's Services, Avondale, PA

Printed in the United States of America

Lake 10 9 8 7 6 5 4 3

This book is printed on acid-free paper.

Contents

User's Guide

This volume is designed to present biographical, critical, and bibliographical information on the author's best-known or most important poems. Following Harold Bloom's editor's note and introduction is a detailed biography of the author, discussing major life events and important literary accomplishments. A thematic and structural analysis of each poem follows, tracing significant themes, patterns, and motifs in the work.

A selection of critical extracts, derived from previously published material from leading critics, analyzes aspects of each poem. The extracts consist of statements from the author, if available, early reviews of the work, and later evaluations up to the present. A bibliography of the author's writings (including a complete list of all books written, cowritten, edited, and translated), a list of additional books and articles on the author and the work, and an index of themes and ideas in the author's writings conclude the volume.

~

Harold Bloom is Sterling Professor of the Humanities at Yale University and Henry W. and Albert A. Berg Professor of English at the New York University Graduate School. He is the author of over 20 books, including *Shelley's Mythmaking* (1959), *The Visionary Company* (1961), *Blake's Apocalypse* (1963), *Yeats* (1970), *A Map of Misreading* (1975), *Kabbalah and Criticism* (1975), *Agon: Toward a Theory of Revisionism* (1982), *The American Religion* (1992), *The Western Canon* (1994), and *Omens of Millennium: The Gnosis of Angels, Dreams, and Resurrection* (1996). *The Anxiety of Influence* (1973) sets forth Professor Bloom's provocative theory of the literary relationships between the great writers and their predecessors. His most recent books include *Shakespeare: The Invention of the Human,* a 1998 National Book Award finalist, and *How to Read and Why,* which was published in 2000.

Professor Bloom earned his Ph.D. from Yale University in 1955 and has served on the Yale faculty since then. He is a 1985 MacArthur Foundation Award recipient, served as the Charles Eliot Norton Professor of Poetry at Harvard University in 1987–88, and has received honorary degrees from the universities of Rome and Bologna. In 1999, Professor Bloom received the prestigious American Academy of Arts and Letters Gold Medal for Criticism.

Currently, Harold Bloom is the editor of numerous Chelsea House volumes of literary criticism, including the series BLOOM'S NOTES, BLOOM'S MAJOR DRAMATISTS, BLOOM'S MAJOR NOVELISTS, MAJOR LITERARY CHARACTERS, MODERN CRITICAL VIEWS, MODERN CRITICAL INTERPRETATIONS, and WOMEN WRITERS OF ENGLISH AND THEIR WORKS.

Editor's Note

My Introduction comments upon all five of the dramatic monologues studied in this volume, emphasizing Browning's masterful ironies, almost Shakespearean in their comprehensiveness.

As there are over twenty-five critical extracts here, I will highlight only a few. The poet Swinburne clarifies "My Last Duchess," while both the novelist George Eliot and the critic-dramatist Oscar Wilde illuminate "Fra Lippo Lippi."

On "Childe Roland to the Dark Tower Came," David V. Erdman provides historical background, after which George M. Ridenour traces the structure of allegory in the poem.

"Andrea del Sarto" enjoys the distinguished reflections of the novelist Henry James and the critic-poet G. K. Chesterton, while Herbert F. Tucker provides more recent insights into the great monologue of the "Imperfect."

With "Caliban Upon Setebos," we are given Walter Bagehot, late Victorian man-of-letters, and the philosopher George Santayana, each investigating links between Browning's nature and his art of the grotesque. J. Hillis Miller, eminent Victorian scholar, unpacks Browning's metaphysics in the poem.

Introduction

HAROLD BLOOM

In proportion to his actual merits of imaginative originality and dramatic power, Robert Browning is probably the most undervalued major poet of the English language, at this time. He is out of fashion, almost totally neglected in our universities, though he still retains favor among common readers who are not swayed by ideologies of gender, race, and cultural politics. Difficult poetry is hardly in demand, and Browning at his subtle best can be quite difficult. The creator of Childe Roland, Andrea del Sarto, and Fra Lippo Lippi was also the re-creator of Shakespeare's Caliban, far more efficaciously than the critics and directors who give us Caliban as a gallant African-American Freedom Fighter.

Browning's dramatic monologue is still an extraordinarily fecund form, as can be seen in the work of Richard Howard and the late Edgar Bowers, as in Robert Frost, T. S. Eliot, and Ezra Pound before them. Tennyson was a rival master of the dramatic monologue, in poems as extraordinary as "Ulysses," "Tithonus," and "Lucretius." But Browning expanded the range and resources of the monologue to the point that it could take on Shakespearean resonances and depths of nihilistic self-deception. The soliloquies of Hamlet, Iago, and Macbeth find their visionary company in the self-explorations of Childe Roland and Andrea del Sarto.

Browning's monologists tell us more than they mean to divulge, and frequently reveal what they themselves do not consciously know. The Duke, speaking in "My Last Duchess," is perfectly candid in observing that he had his "last Duchess" murdered—"I gave commands;/Then all smiles stopped together"—but presumably is not aware that he conveys clinical madness as well as family and personal pride (to call it that, being indistinguishable from his mania).

Childe Roland describes a nightmare landscape, yet we might not see all things deformed and broken had we the misfortune to ride with him. His outrageous question is: "Should I be fit to fail" like his precursors, the band of knights who have preceded him in his quest for the Dark Tower. The quest is for failure, and yet it sublimely succeeds. At the close, Roland stands dauntless, confronting not some nameless ogre but the ring of fire that encircles him, a living flame of all the band of brothers who have been self-betrayed before him. Despair is replayed by the courageous trumpet of a prophecy, as Roland sounds out his fate as his proud motto of self-identification. The final confrontation, and the symbolic journey on his "darkening path," are revealed to be anything but the sickness unto death that Roland believed himself to exemplify. The cost of his confirmation may be his life (we do not know) but his failure is an achieved magnificence, as he sees and *knows* the poet-questers before him. It is as if Browning, who had worshipped Shelley for a lifetime but felt guilty at having abandoned him at the behest of a fierce Evangelical mother, reclaims his Shelleyan, uncompromising heritage in a single epiphany.

The two great matched monologues, "Fra Lippo Lippi" and "Andrea del Sarto," contrast two visions of the artist: hearty naturalist in Lippi and timid self-crippler in Andrea. Browning identifies his own art with Lippi's and portrays Andrea as the compromiser that the husband of Elizabeth Barrett Browning feared to become, had he accepted her influence. And yet both of these grand monologues transcend these implicit self-identifications. Fra Lippo Lippi, though a Carmelite friar, lives what he paints, sensual love:

> I always see the garden and God there
> A-making man's wife: and, my lesson learned,
> The value and significance of flesh,
> I can't unlearn ten minutes afterwards.

Lippi, at one with himself, nevertheless stresses a painterly originality he does not possess. He copies the manner of his teacher Masaccio, the "Hulking Tom" who enters the poem in the verse paragraph commencing at line 270. But, in Lippi's account, Masaccio is the student, not the teacher, a reversal of fact that portrays Lippi's anxiety of influence. Doubtless, Browning hints also at his own continued anxiety in regard to Shelley. Browning's own fear of self-betrayal subtly colors the exquisite monologue by Andrea del Sarto: "A common greyness silvers everything." A great twilight piece, "Andrea del Sarto" is a depiction of knowing self-degradation:

> Ah, but a man's reach should exceed his grasp,
> Or what's a heaven for? All is silver-grey
> Placid and perfect with my art: the worse!

The most grotesque of Browning's masterpieces, "Caliban Upon Setebos," has the audacity to elaborate upon Shakespeare's *The Tempest*. Caliban, painfully meditating upon his mother's god, Setebos, parodies Browning's own humanization of the Evangelical Jesus who was *his* mother's god. But the grim humor of Browning's parody takes its force from elements not wholly ironic, going back as they do to Shakespeare's representation of Caliban's pathos. A composite art emerges, very difficult to describe but unmistakable to hear:

> 'Believeth with the life, the pain shall stop.
> His dam held different, that after death
> He both plagued enemies and feasted friends:
> Idly! He doth His worst in this our life,
> Giving just respite lest we die through pain,
> Saving last pain for worst,—with which, an end. ❀

Biography of
Robert Browning

Robert Browning was born May 7, 1812, in Camberwell, a town near London, to Robert Sr. and Sarah Anna Weidmann Browning. Robert's father worked as a banker but cherished learning, cultivating throughout his life interests in visual art, 18th-century verse, history, and book collecting. Robert Browning Sr.'s library boasted 6,000 volumes on various subjects; this helped support an atmosphere of learning. Sarah Browning had a strong influence on her son's moral and emotional development, and her love of music probably inspired her son's own appreciation. Browning's mother was a devout Christian, and she demanded his regular attendance at church. The Christian orientation Sarah gave her son remained with Robert for the rest of his life.

Browning began his formal education at a local elementary school but was quickly dismissed for being so far ahead of his classmates. After a period of immersion in his father's library, he entered a school in Peckham and studied there until he was fourteen, developing a knowledge of Greek and a taste for the poetry of George Gordon, Lord Byron. While he was at school, 13-year-old Robert wrote a number of poems which he collected and titled *Incondita;* these were never published and were later destroyed by Browning. During his teens Browning also discovered the work of the French philosopher Voltaire and and the English Romantic poet Percy Bysshe Shelley; their work caused him to go through a period of spiritual questioning. Robert's interest in Shelley's poetry would prove to be more than just an adolescent predilection, and much later criticism discusses Shelley's influence on Browning's verse.

Browning's education after leaving school occurred largely at home, where his father taught him Latin and Greek and various tutors instructed him in Italian, French, and music. Browning enrolled to study languages at the new University of London in 1828 but dropped out after only half a year, declaring his intention to become a poet.

In 1833 Browning completed *Pauline,* publication of which was subsidized by an aunt. Apart from a few optimistic reviews, response to the long poem was cold. Among the reviewers was the young John Stuart Mill, who would become a great Victorian philosopher and economist. Browning took Mill's comments to heart, and this probably pointed him toward the dramatic monologue as a poetic form. It is in this form, safe behind the voice of a persona, that Browning created his most characteristic work.

After touring Russia, in 1835 the poet published *Paracelsus*, which earned him recognition among intellectuals like John Forster, Walter Savage Landor, and the aging William Wordsworth, but was another failure financially. Shifting from poetry to drama, Browning wrote the historical play *Strafford* (1837). His fortunes were not any better on the stage than they had been as a poet: *Strafford* was performed only five times.

In 1840, Browning's long poem *Sordello* was published. Seven years in the making, the work shows a poet's conflicted thoughts on the best way to earn renown, through personal action or by the power of poetry. Unfortunately, *Sordello* proved too obscure for his audience, and the work lost him much of the reputation he had gained with *Paracelsus*.

Despite this failure, Browning continued to write verse drama for the stage until 1846. The early 1840s also chronicle the beginning of Browning's shift to a shorter lyric mode, and he published *Dramatic Lyrics* in 1842 and *Dramatic Romances and Lyrics* in 1845, each of which contains enduring work: "My Last Duchess" and "The Pied Piper of Hamelin" appeared in the former, and the latter included "Pictor Ignotus," "The Laboratory," and "The Flight of the Duchess."

Robert Browning had visited Italy in 1838 and he returned there in 1844, the same year a popular English poet named Elizabeth Barrett published her *Poems*. In 1845 Browning wrote Barrett a forthright note of admiration in which he daringly declared that he loved her poetry and loved her too, though they had not yet met. They met later that year, and Robert courted Elizabeth, an invalid, under the watchful eye of her distrustful father. They married in 1846 and the couple went to Paris. From there they visited Marseilles and Pisa, and finally arrived to Florence, where in 1847 they began a fourteen-year stay. While in Florence, the couple developed friendships with the Trollopes, Frederick Tennyson, and Margaret Fuller.

For most of the 1850s Elizabeth's popularity far exceeded Robert's. In 1850 Elizabeth Barrett Browning's greatest work, *Sonnets from the Portuguese*, was published. (Among the sonnets in this collection is one that begins with the line "How do I love thee? Let me count the ways.") The incredible popularity of *Sonnets from the Portuguese* made Elizabeth Barrett Browning one of the foremost English poets of her time. The same year, Robert Browning's long poem *Christmas Eve and Easter Day* sold poorly. The work had probably been inspired by Browning's renewed interest in religion after the death of his mother in 1849. Browning's single best collection of poems, *Men and Women*, was published in 1855.

The couple enjoyed a happy marriage, raising their son Pen in Italy, until Elizabeth died in 1861. Grief-stricken, Browning and Pen left Florence, eventually settling in London, where the poet would remain for the next twenty-six years. With the publication of *Dramatis Personae* in 1864 Browning finally gained recognition as an important poet, but it was not until the 1869 appearance of *The Ring and the Book*, an epic-length poetic work about an ancient murder case, that Browning joined the highest ranks of English poets. Praise for the work was profuse, and in the wake of its reception Browning became a notable socialite. During the summer of 1869 Browning pursued a romance with Louisa Lady Ashburton, a rich widow who rejected his marriage proposal but did not end their affair until 1871.

Browning's success and busy social life did not slow his writing. *Fifine at the Fair* appeared in 1872 and *Red Cotton Night Cap Country* came out the next year. 1875 saw the publication of two works: *Aristophanes' Apology* and *The Inn Album*. Though the works of the 1870s are not as popular today as *Men and Women* or *The Ring and the Book*, they testify to Browning's unflagging creative energy. His final volume, *Asolando*, published in 1889 when the poet had reached the age of 77, is regarded as one of his finest achievements.

For the most part Browning's later life was a comfortable one. The Browning Society, a group dedicated to the poet's work and views, formed in 1881 and may be taken as an indicator of his status as a celebrity. He received honorary degrees from Oxford, Cambridge, and Edinburgh. The deaths of Thomas Carlyle, Matthew Arnold, and Browning's close friend Joseph Milsand during the 1880s made for periods of grief, and Edward Fitzgerald's sour letter about Elizabeth's work, published along with the rest of his correspondence in 1889, provoked an especially bitter response from Browning. But by and large Browning enjoyed his success to the fullest, entertaining friends and writing verse to the very last. In the fall of 1889 Browning traveled to Asolo, Italy, in order to pay respects to several friends. Later he joined his sister in Venice, where he died on December 12, 1889—the same day *Asolando* was published to immediate approbation in London. He was buried later that month in the Poet's Corner in Westminster Abbey. ❋

Thematic Analysis of
"My Last Duchess"

"My Last Duchess" appeared in Browning's first collection of shorter poems, *Dramatic Lyrics* (1842). In the original edition, the poem is printed side-by-side with "Count Gismond" under the heading "Italy and France," and the two poems share a similar concern with issues of aristocracy and honor. "My Last Duchess" is one of many poems by Browning that are founded, at least in part, upon historical fact. Extensive research lies behind much of Browning's work, and "My Last Duchess" represents a confluence of two of Browning's primary interests: the Italian Renaissance and visual art. Both the speaker of the poem and his "last Duchess" closely resemble historical figures. The poem's duke is likely modeled upon Alfonso II, the last Duke of Ferrara, whose marriage to the teenaged Lucrezia de' Medici ended mysteriously only three years after it began. The duke then negotiated through an agent to marry the niece of the Count of Tyrol.

True to the title of the volume in which the poem appears, "My Last Duchess" begins with a gesture performed before its first couplet—the dramatic drawing aside of a "curtain" in front of the painting. From its inception, the poem plays upon the notion of the theatrical, as the impresario duke delivers a monologue on a painting of his late wife to an envoy from a prospective duchess. That the poem constitutes, structurally, a monologue, bears significantly upon its meaning and effects. Browning himself summed up *Dramatic Lyrics* as a gathering of "so many utterances of so many imaginary persons, not mine," and the sense of an authorial presence outside of "My Last Duchess" is indeed diminished in the wake of the control the duke seems to wield over the poem. The fact that the duke is the poem's only voice opens his honesty to question, as the poem offers no other perspective with which to compare or contrast that of the duke. Dependence on the duke as the sole source of the poem invites in turn a temporary sympathy with him, in spite of his outrageous arrogance and doubtlessly criminal past. The poem's single voice also works to focus attention on the duke's character: past deeds pale as grounds for judgment, becoming just another index to the complex mind of the aristocrat.

In addition to foregrounding the monologic and theatrical nature of the poem, the poem's first dozen lines also thematize notions of repetition and sequence, which are present throughout the poem. "That's my last Duchess," the duke begins, emphasizing her place in a series of attachments that presumably include a "first" and a "next." The stagy gesture of drawing aside the curtain is also immanently repeatable: the duke has shown the painting before and will again. Similarly, the duke locates the envoy himself within a sequence of "strangers" who have "read" and been intrigued by the "pictured countenance" of the duchess. What emerges as the duke's central concern—the duchess's lack of discrimination—also relates to the idea of repetition, as the duke outlines a succession of gestures, events, and individuals who "all and each/Would draw from her alike the approving speech." The duke's very claim to aristocratic status rest upon a series—the repeated passing on of the "nine-hundred-years-old name" that he boasts. The closing lines of "My Last Duchess" again suggest the idea of repetition, as the duke directs the envoy to a statue of Neptune: "thought a rarity," the piece represents one in a series of artworks that make up the duke's collection. The recurrent ideas of repetition and sequence in the poem bind together several of the poem's major elements—the duke's interest in making a new woman his next duchess and the vexingly indiscriminate quality of his last one, the matter of his aristocratic self-importance and that of his repugnant acquisitiveness, each of which maps an aspect of the duke's obsessive nature.

This obsessiveness also registers in the duke's fussy attention to his own rhetoric, brought up throughout the poem in the form of interjections marked by dashes in the text. "She had/a heart—how shall I say—too soon made glad," the duke says of his former duchess, and his indecision as to word choice betrays a tellingly careful attitude toward discourse. Other such self-interruptions in the poem describe the duke's uncertainty as to the duchess's too easily attained approval, as well as his sense of being an undiplomatic speaker. On the whole, these asides demonstrate the duke's compulsive interest in the pretence of ceremony, which he manipulates masterfully in the poem. Shows of humility strengthen a sense of the duke's sincerity and frank nature, helping him build a rapport with his audience. The development of an ostensibly candid persona works to cloak the duke's true "object"—the dowry of his next duchess.

Why the duke broaches the painful matter of his sordid past in the first place is well worth considering and yields a rich vein of psychological speculation. Such inquiry should be tempered, however, by an awareness of the duke's overt designs in recounting his past. On the surface, for instance, the poem constitutes a thinly veiled warning: the duke makes a show of his authority even as he lets out some of the rather embarrassing details surrounding his failed marriage. The development of the duchess's seeming disrespect is cut short by the duke's "commands"—almost certainly orders to have her quietly murdered. In the context of a meeting with the envoy of a prospective duchess, the duke's confession cannot but convey a threat, a firm declaration of his intolerance toward all but the most respectful behavior.

But the presence of an underlying threat cannot fully account for the duke's rhetorical exuberance, and the speech the poem embodies must depend for its impetus largely upon the complex of emotional tensions that the memory calls up for the duke. As critic W. David Shaw remarks, the portrait of the last duchess represents both a literal and a figurative "hang-up" for the duke, who cannot resist returning to it repeatedly to contemplate its significance. So eager is the duke to enlarge upon the painting and its poignance that he anticipates and thus helps create the envoy's interest in it, assuming in him a curiousity as to "how such a glance came" to the countenance of the duchess. The duke then indulges in obsessive speculation on the "spot of joy" on the "Duchess' cheek," elaborating different versions of its genesis. Similarly, the duke masochistically catalogues the various occasions the duchess found to "blush" or give praise: love, sunsets, cherries, and even "the white mule/She rode with round the terrace."

Language itself occupies a particularly troubled place in the duke's complex response to his last duchess and her memory. The duke's modesty in declaiming his "skill/In speech" is surely false, as the rhetorical virtuosity of his speech attests. Yet he is manifestly averse to resolving the issue through discussion. In the duke's view, "to be lessoned" or lectured is to be "lessened" or reduced, as his word choice phonetically implies. Rather than belittle himself or his spouse through the lowly practice of negotiation, the duke sacrifices the marriage altogether, treating the duchess's "trifling" as a capital offense. The change the duke undergoes in the wake of disposing of his last duchess is in large part a rhetorical one, as he "now" handles discursively what he once handled with set imperatives.

The last lines of the poem abound in irony. As they rise to "meet/The company below," the duke ominously reminds the envoy that he expects an ample dowry by way of complimenting the "munificence" of the Count. The duke then tells the envoy that not money but the Count's daughter herself remains his true "object," suggesting the idea that the duke's aim is precisely the contrary. The duke's intention to "go/Together down" with the envoy, meant on the surface as a kind of fraternal gesture, ironically underscores the very distinction in social status that it seems to erase. "Innsbruck" is the seat of the Count of Tyrol whose daughter the duke means to marry, and he mentions the bronze statue with a pride that is supposed to flatter the Count. But the lines can also be interpreted as an instance of self-flattery, as Neptune, who stands for the duke, is portrayed in the sculpture as an authorial figure, "taming a sea-horse."

"My Last Duchess" marks an early apex of Browning's art, and some of the elements of the poem—such as the monologue form, the discussion of visual art, and the Renaissance setting—were to become staples of Browning's aesthetic. "My Last Duchess" also inaugurates Browning's use of the lyric to explore the psychology of the individual. As many critics have suggested, character for Browning is always represented as a process, and the attitudes of his characters are typically shown in flux. The duke of "My Last Duchess" stands as a testimony to Browning's ability to use monologue to frame an internal dialogue: the duke talks to the envoy but in effect talks to himself as he compulsively confronts the enigmas of his past. ❀

Critical Views on
"My Last Duchess"

[John Forster (1812–1876) was a prominent historian, biographer and critic in Victorian England. Known chiefly for his *Life of Dickens* (1874), Forster occupied a central position in the literary culture of his time and frequently contributed to journals and newspapers throughout his career. In this review of *Dramatic Lyrics,* Forster discusses Browning's uneven early development while emphasizing that he has only partially realized his potential.]

There was an extremely clever dissertation on Mr Browning's poems in one of the quarterly reviews the other day, in which *Sordello* was recommended as 'a fine mental exercise.' Something of the sort we had said ourselves, and if poetry were exactly the thing to grind professors of metaphysics on, we should pray to Mr Browning for perpetual *Sordellos.* As it is, we are humble enough and modest enough to be more thankful for *Dramatic Lyrics.* The collection before us is welcome for its own sake, and more welcome for its indication of the poet's continued advance in a right direction. Some of this we saw and thanked him for in his *Victor and Charles,* much more in his delightful *Pippa Passes,* and in the simple and manly strain of some of these *Dramatic Lyrics,* we find proof of the firmer march and steadier control. Mr Browning will win his laurel. We were the first to hail his noble start in *Paracelsus*; the *Straffords* and *Sordellos* did not shake our faith in him; and we shall see him reach the goal. ⟨. . .⟩

It is an honourable distinction of Mr Browning that in whatever he writes, you discover *an idea* of some sort or other. You shall have great difficulty in finding it, when he happens to have the humour of obscurity upon him; and there are many of his wilful humours, in which it shall not be worth the search: but any how there it is. He is never a tagger of verses. There is purpose in all he does. Often there is thought of the profoundest kind, often the most exquisite tenderness, his best passages are full of the best Saxon words, and in the art of versification he must be called a master. It is his surpassing facility in this particular, that now and then plays bewildering pranks with his reader's ear—distracting, dazing, and confusing it, in mazes of complicated harmony. On more happy occasions, the flow with which his lines gush forth into the kind of music most appropriate to the thoughts that prompt them, is to us extremely charming; and for the neatness of his rhymes in his lighter efforts, we think that Butler would have hugged him. In a word, Mr Browning is a genuine poet, and only needs to have less misgiving on the subject himself, to win his readers to as perfect a trust, and an admiration with as little alloy in it, as any of his living brethren of the laurel are able to lay claim to.

The *Lyrics*, as their title imports, are for the most part dramatic: full of the quick turns of feeling, the local truth, and the picturesque force of expression, which the stage so much delights in. ⟨. . .⟩

Various is the merit of these various poems: sometimes very grave the faults. But on the whole they confirm what we have said of Mr Browning's genius, and prove that he is fast reclaiming it from the 'vague and formless infinite' of mere metaphysical abstraction.

> —John Forster, "Review of *Dramatic Lyrics*," *The Examiner* (26 November 1842). In *Browning: The Critical Heritage*, ed. Boyd Litzinger and Donald Smalley (London: Routledge and Kegan Paul, 1970): pp. 82–84.

ALGERNON CHARLES SWINBURNE ON BROWNING'S ALLEGED OBSCURITY

[Algernon Charles Swinburne (1837–1909) was a central poet and critic of the Victorian era. His poetry is characteristically marked by profuse melodiousness and prosodic innovation, and his numerous works include *Atalanta and Calydon* (1865), *Poems and Ballads* (1866), and studies of Shakespeare, Blake, and Shelley. In this extract from an essay on George Chapman, Swinburne argues against the common charge that Browning's poetry is too obscure.]

Now if there is any great quality more perceptible than another in Mr. Browning's intellect it is his decisive and incisive faculty of thought, his sureness and intensity of perception, his rapid and trenchant resolution of aim. To charge him with obscurity is about as accurate as to call Lynceus purblind or complain of the sluggish action of the telegraphic wire. He is something too much the reverse of obscure; he is too brilliant and subtle for the ready reader of a ready writer to follow with any certainty the track of an intelligence which moves with such incessant rapidity, or even to realise with what spider-like swiftness and sagacity his building spirit leaps and lightens to and fro and backward and forward as it lives along the animated line of its labour, springs from thread to thread and darts from centre to circumference of the glittering and quivering web of living thought woven from the inexhaustible stores of his perception and kindled from the inexhaustible fire of his imagination. He never thinks but at full speed; and the rate of his thought is to that of another man's as the speed of a railway to that of a wagon or the speed of a telegraph to that of a railway. It is hopeless to enjoy the charm or to apprehend the gist of his writings except with a mind thoroughly alert, an attention awake at all points, a spirit open and ready to be kindled by the contact of the writer's. ⟨. . .⟩

What is important for our present purpose is to observe that this work of exposition by soliloquy and apology by analysis can only be accomplished or undertaken by the genius of a great special pleader, able to fling himself with all his heart and all his brain, with all the force of his intellect and all the strength of his imagination, into the assumed part of his client; to concentrate on the cause in hand his whole power of illustration and illumination, and bring to bear upon one point at once all the rays of his thought in one focus. Apart from his gift of moral imagination, Mr. Browning has in the supreme degree the qualities of a great debater or an eminent leading counsel; his finest reasoning has in its expression and development something of the ardour of personal energy and active interest which inflames the argument of a public speaker; we feel, without the reverse regret of Pope, how many a first-rate barrister or parliamentary tactician has been lost in this poet.

The enjoyment that Browning's best and most characteristic work affords us is doubtless far other than the delight we derive from the purest and highest forms of the lyric or dramatic art; there is a radical difference between the analyst and the dramatist, the pleader and the prophet; it would be clearly impossible for the subtle tongue which can undertake at once the apology and the anatomy of such motives as may be assumed to impel or to support a 'Prince Hohenstiel-Schwangau' on his ways of thought and action, ever to be touched with the fire which turns to a sword or to a scourge the tongue of a poet to whom it is given to utter as from Patmos or from Sinai the word that fills all the heaven of song with the lightnings and thunders of chastisement. But in place of lyric rapture or dramatic action we may profitable enjoy the unique and incomparable genius of analysis which gives to these special pleadings such marvellous life and interest as no other workman in that kind was ever or will ever again be able to give. ⟨. . .⟩

> —Algernon Charles Swinburne, *The Complete Works of Algernon Charles Swinburne*, vol. II, ed. Sir Edmond Gosse and Thomas James Wise (London: William Heinemann Ltd., 1926): pp. 145–46, 149–50.

ROBERT LANGBAUM ON MORAL JUDGMENT IN THE DRAMATIC MONOLOGUE

[Robert Langbaum is Professor Emeritus at the University of Virginia, where he taught English literature. His critical works include *The Modern Spirit* (1970), *The Mysteries of Identity* (1977), and *The Poetry of Experience* (1957), from which this extract is taken. Perhaps the most frequently quoted of Browning's critics, Langbaum here discusses how the formal properties of the dramatic monologue make for a suspension of moral judgment in "My Last Duchess."]

The utter outrageousness of the duke's behaviour makes condemnation the least interesting response, certainly not the response that can account for the poem's success. What interests us more than the duke's wickedness is his immense attractiveness. His conviction of matchless superiority, his intelligence and bland amorality, his poise, his taste for art, his manners—high-handed aristocratic manners that break the ordinary rules and assert the duke's superiority when he is being most solicitous of the envoy, waiving their difference of rank ("Nay, we'll go / Together down, sir"); these qualities overwhelm the envoy, causing him apparently to suspend judgment of the duke, for he raises no demur. The reader is no less overwhelmed. We suspend moral judgment because we prefer to participate in the duke's power and freedom, in his hard core of character fiercely loyal to itself. Moral judgment is in fact important as the thing to be suspended, as a measure of the price we pay for the privilege of appreciating to the full this extraordinary man.

It is because the duke determines the arrangement and relative subordination of the parts that the poem means what it does. The duchess's goodness shines through the duke's utterance; he makes no attempt to conceal it, so preoccupied is he with his own standard of judgment and so oblivious of the world's. Thus the duchess's case is subordinated to the duke's, the novelty and complexity of which engages our attention. We are busy trying to understand the man who can combine the connoisseur's pride in the lady's beauty with a pride that caused him to murder the lady rather than tell her in what way she displeased him, for in that

> would be some stooping; and I choose
> Never to stoop.

The duke's paradoxical nature is fully revealed when, having boasted how at his command the duchess's life was extinguished, he turns back to the portrait to admire of all things its life-likeness:

> There she stands
> As if alive.

This occurs ten lines from the end, and we might suppose we have by now taken the duke's measure. But the next ten lines produce a series of shocks that outstrip each time our understanding of the duke, and keep us panting after revelation with no opportunity to consolidate our impression of him for moral judgment. For it is at this point that we learn to whom he has been talking; and he goes on to talk about dowry, even allowing himself to murmur the hypocritical assurance that the new bride's self and not the dowry is of course his object. It seems to me that one side of the duke's nature is here stretched as far as it will go; the dazzling figure threatens to decline into paltriness admitting moral judgment, when Browning retrieves it with two brilliant strokes. First, there is the lordly waiving of rank's privilege as the duke and the envoy are about to proceed downstairs, and then there is the perfect all-revealing gesture of the last two and a half lines when the duke stops to show off yet another object in his collection: ⟨...⟩

If we allowed indignation, or pity for the duchess, to take over when the duke moves from his account of the murder to admire the life-likeness of the portrait, the poem could hold no further surprises for us; it could not even go on to reinforce our judgment as to the duke's wickedness, since the duke does not grow in wickedness after the account of the murder. He grows in strength of character, and in the arrogance and poise which enable him to continue command of the situation after his confession of murder has threatened to turn it against him. To take the full measure of the duke's distinction we must be less concerned to condemn than to appreciate the triumphant transition by which he ignores clean out of existence any judgment of his story that the envoy might have presumed to invent. We must be concerned to appreciate the exquisite timing of the duke's delay over Neptune, to appreciate its fidelity to the duke's own inner rhythm as he tries once more the envoy's already sorely tried patience, and as he teases the reader too by delaying for a lordly whim the poem's conclusion. This willingness of the reader to understand the duke, even to sympathize with him as a necessary condition of reading the poem, is the key to the poem's form. It alone is responsible for a meaning not inherent in the content itself but determined peculiarly by the treatment.

> —Robert Langbaum, "The Dramatic Monologue: Sympathy versus Judgment," *Robert Browning*, ed. Harold Bloom (New York: Chelsea House, 1985): pp. 29–30, 31.

W. DAVID SHAW ON THE THEATRICALITY OF "MY LAST DUCHESS"

[W. David Shaw, an authority on Victorian literature, teaches English at the University of Toronto. His books include *Tennyson's Style* (1976), *The Lucid Veil: Poetic Truth in the Victorian Age* (1987), and *Elegy and Paradox* (1994). Here Shaw develops a reading of the theatricality of "My Last Duchess," situating the poem within the context of Sigmund Freud's notion of obsession in order to cast light on the force of will that drives the speech.]

Commentators have sensed that the Duke is staging a "show" for the envoy by drawing and closing curtains and speaking rhetorically. George Monteiro, in particular, has stressed the dramatic basis of the Duke's speech: "Virtually a libretto, the Duke's monologue sustains a central metaphor of drama and performance." He begins his play with a curtain, and "sees himself in a dramatic light." But because most critics have paid too little attention to the Duke's language and gestures, they have not generally recognized the full extent to which he is involved in a drama of social pretension—of ceremonious posturing, play acting, and verbal artifice. The ceremony is part of the stagecraft. He was like the producer of a play till life, in the form of his Duchess' admirers, moved into his theatre and set up its counterplay. Isolated by the greedy idolatries of his producer's art, the Duke's theatrical self has fiercely willed the extinction of every other self. Now, in the perfect theatre of the dramatic monologue, with the envoy as his captive audience, the Duke must restage the uneven drama of his domestic life in the form most flattering to his producer's ego. He is at last ready to give the faultless performance which, as we gradually infer, he has never had the absolute mastery to stage in real life. ⟨. . .⟩

The Duke's behavior conforms precisely to Freud's classic analysis of the obsessional neurosis. It transforms and corrects the domestic situation giving rise to his obsession. The ceremonious rhetoric, matchlessly contrived to secure, from the first lordly gesture to the final impudent levity, a breath-taking progression of dramatic shocks, keeps suggesting that the Duke is play acting, and that however reprehensible he may really be, he is not Satanic in the grand Miltonic way he would like the envoy and the reader to believe he is. ⟨. . .⟩ According to Freud, "The actions performed in an obsessional condition are supported by a kind of energy which probably has no counterpart in normal mental life." The Duke makes a tyranny, not only within his own domestic life, but also within the theatrical domain of art. The Duke resembles Browning himself in relation to the reader, and calculates every phrase and gesture that will force his own will or aesthetic intention on the envoy. ⟨. . .⟩

The Duke's spellbinding performance before his auditor enables him to glory in what Kenneth Burke has called "an aesthetic of crime which is infused, however perversely, with the 'mystery' of aristocracy." He represents "aristocratic vice," criminality that has the appeal of dramatic style. This is because Browning has cast the Duke as the outrageous producer of a social play which must bring into harmony with the prejudices of the speaker's own taste every spontaneous action of the Duchess. The Duke's theatrical sense, finely adjusted and revealing no more than a shadow of concern with the nominal purpose of his interview, results in the removal of the speaker from the reader and in the willed isolation of his person. He is the compulsive producer who must re-enact on a stage flattering to his thwarted ego the drama of his past domestic life, and who, with all the craft of the spellbinder's art, deliberately sets out to control the responses of the envoy. The Duke's treatment of his auditor is strikingly rhetorical; he gives evidence of what Burke would call a "pantomimic" morality always on the alert for slight advantages. Even his self-abasement before his visitor is a form of self-exaltation, "the first 'stratagem' of pride."

—W. David Shaw, *The Dialectical Temper: The Rhetorical Art of Robert Browning* (Ithaca, N.Y.: Cornell University Press, 1968): pp. 94, 100–1, 102–3.

LOY D. MARTIN ON THE DRAMATIC MONOLOGUE

[Loy D. Martin has taught English at Stanford University and is the author of *Browning's Dramatic Monologues and the Post-Romantic Subject* (1985). In this extract, Martin addresses the temporal dimension of the dramatic monologue and how it relates to the judgment of the speaker's character in "My Last Duchess."]

The dramatic monologue, in one of its principal functions, creates a poetic moment of a certain duration which is viewed internally and which is contiguous with an implied extra-textural past and future of indefinite extent. The "present" of the dramatic monologue is thus implicitly one open-ended fragment in a succession of fragments which do not, even projectively, add up to a bounded whole. To adopt an immediately relevant linguistic analogy, Browning, by inventing the dramatic monologue, discovered an inclusive form for the manifestation of imperfectivity. ⟨. . .⟩

The technique of provoking unanswered questions, delaying the useful information that answers them as long as possible and then, while supplying that information, raising new questions to start the process all over again, constitutes one of the central rhetorical strategies of the dramatic monologue. The Duchess' portrait is said to be successful because it captures her passion—this we learn in line 8. Not until lines 14–15 does the Duke specify that passion as "joy," and finally, in lines 20–21, we discover that he considers her joy indiscriminate and too easily stimulated. In similar fashion, the Duke's visitor is told in lines 3–4 that Fra Pandolf painted the Duchess' portrait in a day, creating a vague suggestion of haste and carelessness. Despite the assertion that Fra Pandolf was mentioned "by design," however, it is not until lines 20–21 that the issue of the painter's superficiality is taken up again to explain that he has been the Duchess' flatterer. Thus, at all times, the poem offers an incomplete account of situation and character, along with the expectation of subsequent filling in. ⟨. . .⟩

Many critics, even those who disagree with one another, have argued that no moral judgment inheres in the structure of the poem itself. William Cadbury believes the Duke to be an ogre and contends that Browning created him "to prove a point of his own which we learn by applying the standards of an external morality." Others, like Robert Langbaum, dissent, maintaining "that moral judgment does not figure importantly in our response to the duke, that we even identify ourselves with him." In either case, "judgment" is something which exists only outside the poem, and the decision to apply it or not to apply it tends to be a matter of choice for the reader. But the structure of the poem seems to me to entail a serious judgment of character while simultaneously requiring our partial "sympathy" with the Duke as a ratification of that judgment. For we are allowed to see the Duke as he is incapable of seeing his fellow creatures: not as an embodiment of a changeless abstraction (his "nine-hundred-year-old name") but as a living, changing, hesitating human being who is finally knowable only in process and only in a fragmentary way. His fixed vision of his Duchesses, past and future, belies the reality of his own existence, so that the final irony of the poem consists in the fact that his misconception of those around him implies a misconception of the very self he worships. And the triumph of Browning's poem lies in the way it prevents its reader from repeating the Duke's error. Both we and the Duke find a vision of life in a work of art; we as easily as he might say "there *he* stands as if alive." But the meaning would be different. Browning has "made us see," as he was fond of saying the poet can do, and what we "see" is life process, while the Duke in his gallery can see only the motionless dead.

—Loy D. Martin, "The Inside of Time: An Essay on the Dramatic Monologue," *Robert Browning: A Collection of Critical Essays,* ed. Harold Bloom and Adrienne Munich (Englewood Cliffs, N.J.: Prentice Hall, 1979): pp. 65, 72–73, 77–78.

Thematic Analysis of
"Fra Lippo Lippi"

The poem "Fra Lippo Lippi" owes its beginnings to the account given in Giorgio Vasari's *Lives of the Artists* (1568) of a painter-monk of the same name who lived in Florence during the fifteenth century. As the poem reflects, Lippi the historical figure enjoyed the patronage of Cosimo de' Medici (1389–1464), a banker who possessed great political power in the city. The speaker's zeal and manifest unorthodoxy also overlap with those of the apparently spirited Lippi of Renaissance Italy, who was dismissed for misconduct from a rectorship and later eloped with a nun.

The monologue begins as Lippi pleads his case to a group of officers who have caught him in the city's red-light district. Lippi begins his defense by playfully accusing his captors of overzealousness, but then substantiates his defense by referring to his influential patron, "Cosimo of the Medici," which effectively removes him from the grip of the law. Having successfully negotiated the encounter, Lippi takes the opportunity to decry the principle of mindless obedience that led the officers to suspect him: "Zooks, are we pilchards, that they sweep the streets/And count fair prize what comes into their net?" What Lippi objects to is the kind of systematic approach to working that reduces humanity's lot to that of "pilchards" or small fish. The theme of recuperating human integrity at the expense of the prevailing orthodoxy runs throughout the poem.

Having set himself on equal footing with the chief officer, Lippi proceeds to explain himself. Weary with painting "saints and saints/And saints again," Lippi joins ranks with a roving pleasure party, letting himself down with a makeshift "ladder" he creates out of materials in his studio. Like the drinking expedition he sends the officers on, Lippi's outing figures as the counterpart of duty, a break from the painting of saints his job requires. Lippi's rationale, like his ladder, develops out of what is close at hand, and he excuses his lustful pursuits by noting his own physicality: "Come, what am I a beast for?" he asks, suggesting that it is unnatural to ignore completely the body's longings.

Not surprisingly then, it is appetite that leads Lippi into an otherwise unlikely life as a monk. He briefly relates the hardships he lived with early in life, when, parentless, he "starved . . . God knows how, a year or two/On fig-skins, melon-parings, rinds and shucks,/Refuse and rubbish." On the brink of death, he is brought by an aunt "to the convent" where he eats his "first bread that month" as he speaks to the priest, who by contrast is "good" and "fat." The renunciations the monastic life demand pale alongside the renunciation of "the mouthful of bread" that Lippi resolves not to part with: he becomes a monk by default, by following an instinct for self-preservation rather than a spiritual calling.

Lippi's difficult past informs his art. What emerges as a realistic eye inclined to common subjects begins in a youth spent "watching folks' faces to know who will fling" him food—the close observation of manner and character that helped Lippi survive. Under such circumstances, "soul and sense . . . grow sharp alike" and Lippi "learns the look of things." The lessons of his past follow him in his studies at the convent, where his artistic impulse overrides his academic one, as he fills "copy-books" with images of "men's faces" drawn from his experience. Lippi's rebellious spirit pays off as the Prior chooses to keep him and turn his creative abilities to good use, employing him to decorate the chapel.

Lippi's debut as a painter stands in sharp contrast to notions of religious art pervasive at the time. He paints as he sees—not the ideal of a group of solemn penitents on their way to confession, but instead a circle of "good old gossips waiting" to tell their petty wrongs. Though the other monks respond favorably, the Prior— whose name emphasizes the older, "prior" standards according to which he judges Lippi—condemns the work precisely for its accuracy. The "faces, arms, legs and bodies" represented resemble "the true/As much as pea and pea," but such realism distresses the Prior, who sees in it a "devil's-game." As opposed to Lippi's appreciation for the human form and its true dispositions, the prior argues the centrality of the ethereal and the ideal: "Give us no more of body than shows soul!" In the Prior's view, art should inspire praise; moreover, it should do so directly, with exemplary images that the faithful can in turn imitate. Lippi's realism represents a distinct danger for the Prior, as it works to "put all thoughts of praise out of our head/With wonder at lines, colours, and what not."

Lippi stands at the beginning of a new movement in art, and his reflections on the Prior's views amount to a critique of style. He contends that body and soul need not detract from one another, but instead can work in concert when rendered skillfully: the more realistic the body, the clearer the soul becomes. The Prior's views are to Lippi paradoxical, given their supposed basis in the Bible. That God created "man's wife," Eve, from Adam's body, attests to "the value and significance of the flesh" for Lippi, who suggests that if the physical mattered to God, it ought to matter to his followers. The "shapes of things, their colours, lights and shades" being divine in origin are not "to be passed over" en route to the ghostly images the Prior prefers. Lippi delivers a miniature manifesto for his new school of art, the central tenet of which will be to "count it crime/To let truth slip."

Much of the rhetoric of Lippi's presentation focuses on the issue of meaning itself. To assume, like the Prior, the insignificance of the physical, would be to make the world an uninterpretable "blot" or "blank." But for Lippi the created world is rife with significance: "it means intensely, and means good." To bypass the physical would be to risk meddling with meaning itself. By contrast, Lippi would maximize meaning's intensity, advocating a strict adherence to the real, and would have his successors paint things "just as they are," without bias. The physical, for Lippi, becomes the very criterion of meaningfulness.

In spite of his strong opinions, Lippi cannot practice what he preaches for fear of losing business. "They with their Latin"—the church dignitaries—demand from him quite a different kind of artistic production. It is because of having resigned himself, he explains, to delivering the standard subject matter, that he occasionally "play[s] the fooleries" the police "catch [him] at." To "make amends" for his misconduct, Lippi plans to oblige his superiors by composing his next work in strict accordance with their preferences. A sense of irony pervades the account of the projected work, which will include a "bowery flowery angel-brood" and "of course, a saint or two." The hyperbole of the former phrase and the dismissive tone of the latter illustrate Lippi's attitude, which is one of perfunctory compliance.

But the Lippi that refuses to be reconciled to such orthodoxy emerges toward the end of the monologue, where he narrates a mischievous plan to indulge his own notions of what art should be, even as he resigns himself to the expectations of others. The painting, otherwise the very embodiment of the prevailing views of religious art, will also include, preposterously, the figure of Lippi himself, "mazed, motionless and moonstruck" in the "pure company" of saints and angels. The justification for painting himself into the picture Lippi puts in the mouth of a "sweet angelic" girl of his own creation: "brother Lippo" too has his value, as he is, after all, the creator of the work he inhabits.

Critics have found an allegorical element in the sub-narrative Lippi appends to his plans for the painting. The "celestial presence" of the girl could represent the muse, while the "hot-head husband" that "pops" in suddenly might figure a prior artist, someone opposed to Lippi's new aesthetic of the real. What emerges without question from the passage is a concern related to Browning's professed interest in the imperfect. That the poem's speaker trails off into a highly private vision of the work and its reception emphasizes a sense of incompleteness, a sense that meaning in art is never wholly contained but implicates the audience, the artist, and his precursors in a complicated web of relations. "There's the grey beginning" Lippi proclaims at the end of the poem, alluding to the dawn as he locates the poem within the context of the temporal, that which, like his art, never quite perfects or completes itself. ❀

Critical Views on
"Fra Lippo Lippi"

GEORGE ELIOT ON BROWNING'S ORIGINALITY

[George Eliot (1819–1880) was the pseudonym of Mary Ann Cross, one of the greatest Victorian novelists. Her works include *Adam Bede* (1859), *The Mill on the Floss* (1860), *Silas Marner* (1861), and *Middlemarch* (1871–2). Eliot, a realist, balanced an attention to the aesthetic aspect of writing with a deeply moral sensibility. In this extract from her review of *Men and Women,* Eliot focuses on the originality of Browning's work while emphasizing that Browning's artistic limits are bound up with the sense of authorial exertion that lies behind the poems.]

To read poems is often a substitute for thought: fine-sounding conventional phrases and the sing-song of verse demand no co-operation in the reader; they glide over his mind with the agreeable unmeaningness of 'the compliments of the season', or a speaker's exordium on 'feelings too deep for expression.' But let him expect no such drowsy passivity in reading Browning. Here he will find no conventionality, no melodious commonplace, but freshness, originality, sometimes eccentricity of expression; no didactic laying-out of a subject, but dramatic indication, which requires the reader to trace by his own mental activity the underground stream of thought that jets out in elliptical and pithy verse. To read Browning he must exert himself, but he will exert himself to some purpose. If he finds the meaning difficult of access, it is always worth his effort—if he has to dive deep, 'he rises with his pearl.' Indeed, in Browning's best poems he makes us feel that what we took for obscurity in him was superficiality in ourselves. We are far from meaning that all his obscurity is like the obscurity of the stars, dependent simply on the feebleness of men's vision. On the contrary, our admiration for his genius only makes us feel the more acutely that its inspirations are too often straitened by the garb of whimsical mannerism with which he clothes them. This mannerism is even irritating sometimes, and should at least be kept under restraint in *printed* poems, where the writer is not merely indulging his own vein, but is avowedly appealing to the mind of his reader.

Turning from the ordinary literature of the day to such a writer as Browning, is like turning from Flotow's music, made up of well-pieced shreds and patches, to the distinct individuality of Chopin's Studies or Schubert's Songs. Here, at least, is a man who has something of his own to tell us, and who can tell it impressively, if not with faultless art. There is nothing sickly or dreamy in him: he has a clear eye, a vigorous grasp, and courage to utter what he sees and handles. His robust energy is informed by a subtle, penetrating spirit, and this blending of opposite qualities gives his mind a rough piquancy that reminds one of a russet apple. His keen glance pierces into all the secrets of human character, but, being as thoroughly alive to the outward as to the inward, he reveals those secrets, not by a process of dissection, but by dramatic painting. ⟨...⟩

Browning has no soothing strains, no chants, no lullabys; he rarely gives voice to our melancholy, still less to our gaiety; he sets our thoughts at work rather than our emotions. But though eminently a thinker, he is as far as possible from prosaic; his mode of presentation is always concrete, artistic, and, where it is most felicitous, dramatic. Take, for example, 'Fra Lippo Lippi,' a poem at once original and perfect in its kind. The artist-monk, Fra Lippo, is supposed to be detected by the night-watch roaming the streets of Florence, and while sharing the wine with which he makes amends to the Dogberrys for the roughness of his tongue, he pours forth the story of his life and his art with the racy conversational vigour of a brawny genius under the influence of the Care-dispeller. ⟨...⟩

But we must also say that though Browning never flounders helplessly on the plain, he rarely soars above a certain table-land—a footing between the level of prose and the topmost heights of poetry. He does not take possession of our souls and set them aglow, as the greatest poets—the greatest artists do. We admire his power, we are not subdued by it. Language with him does not seem spontaneously to link itself into song, as sounds link themselves into melody in the mind of the creative musician; he rather seems by his commanding powers to compel language into verse. He has *chosen* verse as his medium; but of our greatest poets we feel that they had no choice: Verse chose them. Still we are grateful that Browning chose this medium: we would rather have 'Fra Lippo Lippi' than an essay on Realism in Art; we would rather have 'The Statue and the Bust' than a three-volumed novel with the same moral; we would rather have 'Holy Cross-Day' than 'Strictures on the Society for the Emancipation of the Jews.'

—George Eliot, unsigned review in *The Westminster Review* 65 (January 1856). Reprinted in *Browning: The Critical Heritage*, ed. Boyd Litzinger and Donald Smalley (London: Routledge and Kegan Paul, 1970): pp. 174–77.

OSCAR WILDE ON BROWNING AS A WRITER OF FICTION

[Novelist, playwright, and essayist Oscar Wilde (1854–1900) was a central figure in fin de siècle British culture and a leading spokesperson for aestheticism. His works include *The Picture of Dorian Gray* (1891) and *The Importance of Being Earnest* (1895). In this assessment of Browning, Wilde discusses the narrative and psychological aspects of Browning's poetry.]

Taken as a whole, the man was great. He did not belong to the Olympians, and had all the incompleteness of the Titan. He did not survey, and it was but rarely that he could sing. His work is marred by struggle, violence, and effort, and he passed not from emotion to form, but from thought to chaos. Still, he was great. He has been called a thinker, and was certainly a man who was always thinking, and always thinking aloud; but it was not thought that fascinated him, but rather the processes by which thought moves. It was the machine he loved, not what the machine makes. The method by which the fool arrives at his folly was so dear to him as the ultimate wisdom of the wise. So much, indeed, did the subtle mechanism of mind fascinate him that he despised language, or looked upon it as an incomplete instrument of expression. ⟨. . .⟩

There are moments when he wounds us by monstrous music. Nay, if he can only get his music by breaking the strings of his lute, he breaks them, and they snap in discord, and no Athenian tettix, making melody from tremulous wings, lights on the ivory horn to make the movement perfect or the interval less harsh. Yet, he was great: and though he turned language into ignoble clay, he made from it men and women that live. He is the most Shakespearian creature since Shakespeare. If Shakespeare could sing with myriad lips, Browning could stammer through a thousand mouths. Even now, as I am speaking, and speaking not against him but for him, there glides through the room the pageant of his persons. There, creeps Fra Lippo Lippi with his cheeks still burning from some girl's hot kiss. There, stands dread Saul with the lordly male-sapphires gleaming in his turban. Mildred Tresham is there, and the Spanish monk, yellow with hatred, and Blougram, and the Rabbi Ben Ezra, and the Bishop of St. Praxed's. The spawn of Setebos gibbers in the corner, and Sebald, hearing Pippa pass by, looks on Ottima's haggard face, and loathes her and his own sin and himself. Pale as the white satin of his doublet, the melancholy king watches with dreamy treacherous eyes too loyal Strafford pass to his doom, and Andrea shudders as he hears the cousin's whistle in the garden, and bids his perfect wife go down. Yes, Browning was great. And as what will he be remembered? As a poet? Ah, not as a poet! He will be remembered as a writer of fiction, as the most supreme writer of fiction, it may be, that we have ever had. His sense of dramatic situation was unrivalled, and, if he could not answer his own problems, he could at least put problems forth. Considered from the point of view of a creator of character he ranks next to him who made Hamlet. Had he been articulate he might have sat beside him. The only man living who can touch the hem of his garment is George Meredith. Meredith is a prose-Browning, and so is Browning. He used poetry as a medium for writing in prose.

—Oscar Wilde, "The True Function and Value of Criticism," *Nineteenth Century* 28 (July 1890). Reprinted in *Browning: The Critical Heritage*, ed. Boyd Litzinger and Donald Smalley (London: Routledge and Kegan Paul, 1970): pp. 524–26.

JAMES RICHARDSON ON THE DYNAMIC RHETORIC OF "FRA LIPPO LIPPI"

[James Richardson is a professor of English at Princeton University, where he teaches Victorian and contemporary poetry, as well as creative writing. His works include *Vanishing Lives* (1988) and three collections of poetry: *Reserva-*

tions (1977), *Second Guesses* (1984), and *As If* (1992). In this extract from *Thomas Hardy: The Poetry of Necessity* (1977), Richardson reads "Fra Lippo Lippi" in the context of Shelleyan Romanticism, examining the anxieties that underlie the speaker's energetic rhetoric.]

Sexual timidity is not, or not obviously, the problem of "Fra Lippo Lippi," and Lippo himself is so ebullient and convincing that it is hard to see that there is another side to the question he raises. His garrulousness, however, shades into overkill, and if he more than convinces the reader of the excusability of his foray into the Italian spring, he does not seem to convince himself of the propriety of what his excursion *represents* for his art. For though Lippo seems completely reconciled to his immersion in life, it is only because he conveniently displaces his anxieties (the same anxieties displayed in "Pictor Ignotus") onto the gray authority figures of his apprenticeship:

> I'm my own master, paint now as I please—
> Having a friend, you see, in the Corner-house!
> Lord, it's fast holding by the rings in front—
> Those great rings serve more purposes than just
> To plant a flag in, or tie up a horse!
> And yet the old schooling sticks, the old grave eyes
> Are peeping o'er my shoulder as I work,
> The heads shake still—"It's art's decline, my son!
> You're not of the true painters, great and old . . ."

Part of Lippo really believes in this decline or diminution, and the moral is that no one "paints as he pleases" because no one can be absolutely certain what pleases him. Despite his protestations to the contrary, Lippo, like the pseudo-Prometheans, worries that he may be sucked into the vortex of the fleshly particular, that through his submission to the possibilities of life he may lose its essence and his own identity. He is *not* his own master because he is still in rebellion against his own fears. He yearns for certainty:

> all I want's the thing
> Settled forever one way. As it is,
> You tell too many lies and hurt yourself:
> You don't like what you only like too much,
> You do like what, if given at your word,
> You find abundantly detestable.
> For me, I think I speak as I was taught;
> I always see the garden and God there

A-making man's wife: and my lesson learned,
The value and significance of flesh,
I can't unlearn ten minutes afterwards.

Lippo's attribution of his confusion to his social conformity is, of course, an oversimplification. It is in fact the result of a genuine and inescapable self-division, and he is compelled to rationalize his interest in the human body in the same terms Browning uses to justify his fascination with the individual human character. Still, Lippo, in contrast to Andrea del Sarto and the painter of "Pictor Ignotus," is a live artist. Accordingly, his compromise is dynamic, and he does not allow himself to find the fatal certainty he seeks. His formulations, like Browning's, are only momentary crystallizations. In a poetry of divided awareness, all approximations of certainty gather into themselves the element of jest or self-deception and become mere rationalizations, but Lippo's vitality transcends both his rationalizations and his misgivings.

—James Richardson, *Thomas Hardy: The Poetry of Necessity* (Chicago: University of Chicago Press, 1977): pp. 50–51.

HERBERT F. TUCKER ON TRADITION AND ORIGINALITY

[Herbert F. Tucker is a professor of English at the University of Virginia, where he teaches Victorian literature. In addition to *Browning's Beginnings: The Art of Disclosure* (1980), from which this extract is taken, Tucker has published *Critical Essays on Alfred Lord Tennyson* (1998) and *A Companion to Victorian Literature and Culture* (1999). Here Tucker discusses the dialectic between artistic tradition and originality in "Fra Lippo Lippi."]

In "Andrea del Sarto" and "A Toccata of Galuppi's," Browning plays a speaker's sterile assurance of meaning against his buried but unquiet consciousness of better possibilities, possibilities that each speaker denies to himself, "grown old," and attributes instead to figures of youth, to Rafael or to the Venetian lovers. In "Fra Lippo Lippi" (1855), Browning gives the stage to such a figure of youth, a painter as aware of his own position at the beginning of a new movement in art as he is aware "that the morning-star's about to shine." The interest of Fra Lippo's monologue, and particularly of the theory of artistic representation that he expounds, lies in the stratagems through which this youthful awareness is preserved. Like Andrea del Sarto and the speaker in "A Toccata of Galuppi's," Lippo quarrels with tendencies in himself. Although his quarrel moves in the contrary direction to theirs, he too uses lay figures—notably, as spokesman for prior masters in painting, the aptly named "Prior" of the Carmelite cloister—as determinants of his later and younger position, as guarantors of his precious sense of standing at a beginning.

Fra Lippo's escape from the clutches of the police into "the grey beginning" of dawn is only the last of the series of escapes from enclosures external and internal that make up his story. G. Wilson Knight writes that in this poem Browning is "fighting for physical reality and vitality as against a premature spiritualizing of the human." This remark illuminates the poem's implicit analogy between the relation of body to soul and the relation of an artifact to it's meaning: Lippo's defense of pictorial realism is a fight for the independence of art from a premature determination of its meaning. It will not be disputed that Fra Lippo's aesthetic opinions are ultimately Browning's, but Browning keeps his poem human and defends it against hasty disclosure of those opinions by letting Lippo gradually work them out for himself. Over the course of the monologue, Lippo emerges from the enclosures of received opinions into his own as an artist who has broken "out of bonds." ⟨. . .⟩

If Lippo is to further the history of art by making paintings that mean in his own different way, he must bear tradition in mind. He must anticipate the tendency of past works suddenly to reappear in works of the present, their tendency in any age to burst into the house of contemporary art, claim a husband's rights, and assert control over works that have aspired to be modern. Otherwise the game will be up; for Lippo to believe in the security of "all the doors being shut" against the incursions of artistic orthodoxy will be to paint himself into a corner of another man's heaven. By fastening the door against tradition and ignoring it, an artist only hastens its return to govern his work in some "wholly unexpected" way that he is powerless to change. In closing his parable, Lippo reintroduces the note of anxiety as a reminder of the vigilant defense, the expectation of the unforeseen, which has motivated his flagrantly improvisatory monologue. When he dismisses the police by saying, "I know my own way back," he means that his own way forward, towards the beginning of a new art, lies through a continuing engagement with the art of the past. Fra Lippo's surest augury of success in this engagement comes with a Paracelsan vision of his successors: "Oh, oh, / It makes me mad to see what men shall do / And we in our graves!" He asserts his place in a living tradition by anticipating his future status as a past master, a "hothead husband" of the muse in his own right.

—Herbert F. Tucker, *Browning's Beginnings: The Art of Disclosure* (Minneapolis: University of Minnesota Press, 1980): pp. 201, 208.

ISOBEL ARMSTRONG ON THE NOTION OF REPRESENTATION

[Isobel Armstrong is a professor of English at Birkbeck College, University of London. Her publications include *Victorian Scrutinies* (1972), *Sense and Sensibility* (1994), and *Women's Poetry in the Enlightenment* (1999) among others. In this extract from *Victorian Poetry: Poetry, Poetics and Politics* (1993), Armstrong discusses the complex way in which the poem stages an ironic and paradoxical inquiry into the idea of representation itself.]

Once incongruously part of the religious scene in monk's habit with 'the rope that goes all round' (the rope that circumscribes, as the picture does, and the rope that throttles, the hangman's rope), however, the painter is subject to the conventions of the picture's world and frozen in it—'Mazed, motionless and moonstruck.' But simply because it *is* a picture he can get out of it—he attempts, with 'blushing face' (embarrassment and lust) to 'shuffle sideways': a sideways shuffle is all that one can attempt on a flat, one-dimensional canvas, but it also marks the obliquity of vision to which all perception is subject, in or out of art. Half in, half out of the picture, the painter of it ventriloquises the speech of the woman who is an angel in the picture, representing God, and the woman who is posing for the representation of an angel outside the picture. One object of the painter's creation speaks to another, God, and blasphemously reverses the order of theological creation by giving the power of origination to the painter—'He made you and devised you': a representation of God who makes man is told by an artist's creation that a man has represented God making man representing God. The return of representation upon itself is endless. But the painter does get out of the picture, and, 'all the doors being shut,' makes love—with the angel who is a woman representing an angel. The doors of the non-fictional church are closed (but of course it is a fiction of Browning's poem) against the outside world as the picture is closed against it. *'Iste perfecit opus'*, says the 'angel' via Lippi or Lippi via the 'angel,' outrageously appropriating the language of creation.

But the picture is not 'finished.' It has a special status as a deliberately made representation which sets it off from other forms of representation; it is a construction which can, despite and with all the limits of the distorted gaze of perception which construes it in terms of its own categories of thought and experience, become the object of analysis—even if you have made it yourself. Nevertheless, the gaze is implicated in the picture, embroiled in it. Even when the painter has 'escaped' from the picture the closure which marks off painting from 'life' is incomplete. The picture has repercussions in experience. Its idealised representation both represses and arouses desire, transmutes it and produces it. Lippi plays 'hot cockles' with the 'angel' in reaction to his own picture, and this has further social repercussions as the 'hothead husband,' inflamed with anger, desire and the rage of flouted legal possession, breaks through the closed doors of the church to claim his domestic angel in the house, asserting the property rights of marriage: an *imagined* scene about the *material* effects of imagination.

The ambiguous status of the constructed aesthetic object or fiction, its reflexivity and the embroilments of its circularity, its self-subversion and subversion, indirect or direct, its ideological nature and the repercussions it has beyond itself, all these are figured in Lippi's problematical inside-outside relation to the picture. He can get neither fully inside nor fully outside it. But what is clear is that as an object of contemplation the picture has entered the world. There is a double mediation between picture and world, world and picture in an endless reactive chain. ⟨. . .⟩

Paradoxically, if linguistic fictions are never exact, then the more exactly they are considered the more richly they can be comprehended. Language is at the heart of ideological misprision and creativity. Language, that indispensable and elusively ambiguous entity, is the material of our inexhaustible fictions, and calls forth all the resources of an equally inexhaustible hermeneutic process. The waywardly eclectic and omnivorously logophiliac inventiveness of Browning's poetry declares itself insistently, almost raucously, with a kind of ravenous energy which asks to be confronted.

—Isobel Armstrong, *Victorian Poetry: Poetry, Poetics and Politics* (London: Routledge, 1993): pp. 297–98, 299.

Thematic Analysis of
"Childe Roland to the Dark Tower Came"

Browning confessed a certain pride in having written "Childe Roland to the Dark Tower Came," which he composed in a single day. It is now probably his most often read poem. The poem takes its title from Edgar's song in Act III, scene four of Shakespeare's *King Lear*: "Childe Roland to the dark tower came,/His word was still, 'Fie foh and fum,/I smell the blood of a British man.'" Edgar's "song" follows upon a speech in which Edgar, disguised as the crazed beggar Poor Tom, laments his status by describing a journey that resonates with the ruined quest that Browning's Roland makes: "Who gives anything to poor Tom? whom the foul fiend hath led through fire and through flame, through [ford] and whirlpool, o'er bog and quagmire . . . made him proud of heart, to ride on a bay-trotting horse over four-inched bridges, to course his own shadow for a traitor." Shakespeare may have supplied the poem's immediate context, but critics have come up with scores of additional sources, Biblical and Romantic, medieval and metaphysical. Still, Edgar's speech and song do locate a number of the poem's overt concerns, including the notion of the grotesque, the significance of landscape, the question of purposelessness, and, most importantly, the notion of the failed quest.

The "foul fiend" Edgar speaks of prefigures the presence of Browning's "hoary cripple," whose encounter with Roland marks the beginning of the poem. The meeting sets in motion a motif of suspicion that recurs throughout the poem. The visage of the cripple works in grotesque concert, provoking a kind of paranoia in Roland, who cannot help but notice the stranger's crooked look and twisted mouth. But from the very first Roland is ready to second guess himself: his sense of being lied to is a "first" thought that will be succeeded by a series of revisions. The first stanza also opens Roland's own veracity to question: does the possessive "mine" refer only to Roland's eye, or does it refer to a falsehood he himself has told the cripple? Are the two trading lies or glances or both as they angle for the upper hand?

What this initial concern with the matter of suspicion points to is the larger issue of reading or interpretation. Roland's manifest anxiety stems from the question of how to read the man's "word" and countenance, an inquiry which in turn gives rise to the question of what precisely he is doing, "posted there" alone in the "dusty" wasteland. Though Roland suspects betrayal, he "acquiescingly" turns as the cripple directs him, thus establishing one of the poem's characteristic movements. Roland is an obsessive reader/interpreter throughout his journey, as if what he gleaned from his close observations would serve him. But here as elsewhere in "Childe Roland," he quests onward not because of what his inquiries have shown him, but rather in spite of what they have failed to show him. "Neither pride/Nor hope" compels Roland on his journey, but rather a somewhat perverse "gladness that some end might be."

Ironically, the "joy success would bring" possesses no attraction for Roland; indeed, this seems to be beyond his capacity to handle. "Failure" draws him on, insofar as it represents an end to his "worldwide wandering." "Child Roland" is a lyric narrative obsessed with teleology—the philosophy of ends. Roland compares himself to a "sick man" who aims only "not to shame" the "tender love" of friends to whom he has already bid farewell, by "stay[ing] alive." By focusing on the end in itself as his goal, Roland's story turns the typical notion of the quest upside down. Remembering the knights who came before him, Roland oddly determines "that to fail as they seemed best." In Roland's inverted version of the quest, to be fit to fail ironically represents a kind of triumph.

The poem's first movement thus closes with Roland's turning from his grisly interlocutor onto "the path" he points to the Dark Tower. As in "Andrea del Sarto" the time is twilight. As the day draws "to its close," Roland fancies the sunset resembles an ominous "red leer," marking the reinitiation of a readerly interest in his surroundings. The "plain" itself, blank though it is, Roland succeeds in suspecting of designs: that it will "catch its estray" means both that it reflects the sun's ray and also that it closes on the "estray" or errant questor who crosses it.

The middle phase of the poem is largely descriptive, as Roland recounts some of the features of the "grey plain" he makes a way across. Landscape occupies a central position in the poem, creating a grim ambience that both reflects and determines Roland's state of mind. Strangely, the landscape acquires a kind of agency: it is, after all, the very boundlessness of the plain that draws Roland onward: "nought else remained to do" but continue. Yet the plain also functions to isolate Roland's radical willfulness, how he persists in pushing onward in spite of the potentially endless tract before him.

The catalogue of features of the "starved ignoble nature" Roland meets is not an unbiased one. Instead of merely noting the sparse vegetation he finds, he interprets it, imputing for example a jealousy to the "bents" or reeds to explain why no "ragged thistle-stalk" ever "pushed" up "above its mates." Similarly, the grass is not simply "scant," but grows like "hair/In leprosy." Roland accounts for the whole of the dreadful scene by imagining a speech made by "Nature," who declares that only "the last Judgment's fire" can "cure this place."

Directing his thoughts inward in search of solace or rejuvenation, Roland finds only memories of his friends' past failures. "Cuthbert's reddening face" comforts Roland only until he recalls the "one night's disgrace" that ruined the warrior. Remembering "Giles," another member of "'The Band,'" likewise brings comfort only until his having become a "poor traitor" resurfaces. Nothing within or without avails Roland, who finally prefers the eerie present of the plain to the sad past he calls up.

Throughout Roland's observations in this section of the poem lies evidence of his will in the form of a kind of heedlessness he adopts when confronted by the inexplicable. Roland reads the landscape, but where he strikes upon a conundrum he does not pause but pushes on. The "stiff blind horse" he sees stands "stupefied," but "however he came there," it is no matter to Roland, who means to bring his quest to its end. In the same way, "whate'er" wrong the river might have done the "scrubby alders" is finally unimportant: like the river itself Roland is "deterred no whit."

The imagery the landscape evokes becomes increasingly nightmarish. Roland imagines a battle to explain the much-trampled shore he discovers as he fords the river. The second movement of the poem concludes as Roland, cued by the sudden and ominous flight of "a great black bird," becomes aware that "the plain had given place/All round to mountains." The nightmare of the plain's terrifying boundlessness yields to the "bad dream" of enclosure, as "in the very nick/of giving up" comes "a click/As when a trap shuts." Though he has spent "a life training for the sight" of the Dark Tower, Roland is shocked to find it directly in front of him, in the midst of the mountains.

It would not be out of line to wonder why Roland does not immediately recognize the tower. Is it really because he is a "Dunce" or "Dotard" that he is at first ignorant of it, or is it possible that the obsessively observant Roland suffers a blindness born of a desire not to see what lies clearly before him? Such questions are worth raising, if only because Roland himself attempts to analyze the momentary lapse of his senses, asking "Not see?" and "Not hear?" in succession, but drawing no adequate conclusion. Roland allegorizes his ignorance to that of a "shipman" who learns from the "mocking elf" of the storm where dangers lurk only when they can no longer be avoided.

The third and final phase of the poem, which begins with Roland's sudden recognition of the tower, thematizes the notion of belatedness. Like the shipman, Roland learns too late to have the chance to change his course. More importantly, Roland is the last and thus the latest in a series of similar quest figures—"all the lost adventurers" whose previous exploits he is so abundantly aware of. Roland's past frames the present, limiting or determining it, just as the past questors in the poem constitute a "living frame" for him, who, like them, will in a "moment" be "lost, lost!"

Critics have noted Browning's ties to Charles Dickens and Franz Kafka, and "Childe Roland to the Dark Tower Came" epitomizes both the grotesque element that links Browning to Dickens, and the concern with inevitability that connects him to Kafka. The poem also exemplifies Browning's penchant for exploring the realm of the psychological. Roland's journey is as much concerned with the physical as with the mental, and the two often blur together as his senses yield to his anxieties. Like "Andrea del Sarto," "Childe Roland" elaborates a vision of an individual who would lay claim to his destiny, however dismal it seems. Together, the two poems stand as Browning's most fully realized attempts to work out the dialectic between fate and the will. ❀

Critical Views on
"Childe Roland to the Dark Tower Came"

DAVID MASSON ON THE SURREAL IN "CHILDE ROLAND"

[David Masson (1822–1907) taught literature at Edinburgh University and edited *Macmillan's Magazine* but is known chiefly as a biographer, and his six volume *Life of Milton* (1859–80) is considered a standard. In this extract from a review of *Men and Women*, Masson notes Browning's genius for recreating characters from history and then considers, by way of contrast, "Childe Roland to the Dark Tower Came," a poem that resides wholly within the realm of the surreal.]

In the art of character-painting, as we have said, in the power of throwing himself into states of mind and trains of circumstance the most alien from our present habits, in the intuitive faculty of reconceiving the most peculiar and obsolete modes of thinking, he ranks as a master. Generally, as we have seen, when he exercises his genius in this manner, he works on a basis of history, adopting a story, or appropriating a character, or at least borrowing a hint from the actual records of the past ages of the world; and almost always when he does so we are struck by the strange selection he makes. It is from the bye-laws of history, or, at least, from what are reckoned such, that he derives the hints on which he proceeds; or, if ever he comes upon the great broad track familiar to the traditions of common men, he is seen approaching it by some unexpected bye-path. ⟨. . .⟩

But Mr. Browning, though he usually exercises his imagination in giving body and expansion to some hint furnished by the actual world of history, can yet, when he chooses, fling reality and history aside altogether, and revel, as well as any poet, in a world of shifting allegoric shapes and sounds and phantasies, where nothing is fixed and nothing literal. This is proved by more than one piece in the present volume, but above all by the one entitled 'Childe Roland to the Dark Tower Came.' Perhaps, indeed, taking the *kind* of the poetry here attempted into account, as well as the success of the attempt *in* that kind, this poem deserves all in all to be regarded as the greatest thing in the volumes. The notion of the poem, as in Tennyson's *Mar-*

iana, is that of expanding one of those snatches of old ballad and allusion which have such a mystic effect in Shakespeare. 'Childe Roland to the Dark Tower Came' is one such snatch of old song quoted by Edgar in *Lear;* and Mr. Browning offers us *his* imaginative rendering of these gloomy hieroglyphic words. The phantasy is one of the most wild and ghastly within the range of our literature, with more of sheer terror in it than in any corresponding phantasy in Spenser. . . .

If this piece be not poetry, we do not know what is. It is poetry of the highest symbolic kind, and we have reserved it to the last among our quotations, as being the farthest removed in its nature of all the pieces in the volumes from the domain of the mere understanding. How it holds the imagination, and is felt to be coherent and significant in meaning, though no one will venture to explain what the meaning is!

—David Masson, review of *Men and Women* in *The British Quarterly Review* 28 (January 1856). Reprinted in *Browning: The Critical Heritage,* ed. Boyd Litzinger and Donald Smalley (London: Routledge and Kegan Paul, 1970): pp. 180, 181.

David V. Erdman on the Background of "Childe Roland"

[David V. Erdman has published extensively on William Blake and has edited *Blake's Visionary Forms* (1970), *The Illuminated Blake* (1974), and *Blake and his Bibles* (1990) among many other works. In this extract from his essay "Browning's Industrial Nightmare" (1957), Erdman reads "Childe Roland to the Dark Tower Came" within the social and political context of mid-century Paris where Browning wrote the poem, finding evidence of veiled concerns with the civil issues of the time.]

Since the subsidence of the Browning Societies there has been a tacit agreement among critics not to allegorize the poem—though it may "be read on several levels of meaning"—but to look about in Browning's previous experience for the various unapprehended ingredients of this compelling vision: *Lear*, Keats, folklore, books on landscape painting—and Browning's striving with obstacles in his wooing of Ba and the muse. I have no quarrel here except with the assumption that Browning's experience and awareness were limited to booklore and the hazards of essentially private and personal quests. I wish not simply to add "The Cry of the Children" to the list of his sources but to call attention to the overlooked social and political components of the motifs of this wasteland poem and to press the necessary assumption that Browning's mind was somehow haunted by the cries of competitive struggle, the publicized wretchedness of workers in mines and mills, and even the spectre of anarchy around the next foothill ⟨. . .⟩

On the simplest level, "Childe Roland" is the narrative soliloquy of a weary warrior on a vaguely explained and perhaps vaguely comprehended Quest traversing a waste land, the vegetation and contours of which menace and puzzle him. He is confident of failure yet worries about whether he will even prove "fit" for that—an ironic twist to the usual theme of fruitless striving. Just as he finds himself at the end of "Progress this way," he sees that he has been walking into a "trap" which *is* simultaneously his goal and his end, the Dark Tower, elaborately symbolic of blind violence and brute force. He had been searching for the Tower, and he recognizes its blind squat turret as appropriate to "the fool." We gather that the aim of "The Band" engaged in this quest (all now "lost" leaders but Roland) has been to find and confront the fool, but that this aim is fully recognized only too late, when the fool is unassailable and all the crusaders have been disgraced or have turned traitor. Our hero has at least the satisfaction of having walked on into the ambush: a shipman has a similar satisfaction (we are told) when he finds the "unseen shelf" by striking on it with the blow that wrecks his ship. ⟨. . .⟩

Within the love poem, and in his attitude toward the quest poem, the poet manages to shrug off the dark implications, to dissociate himself from the baffling aberrations of a nation destroying itself. For Browning, like his projected Childe recently arrived from "world-wide wandering," does not stand forth to draw sword—against whom, after all?—but only to utter his momentary vision of betrayal. Nevertheless he arranges his uncomprehended vision in the form of an unsolved riddle, whose burning question is: How did things come to such a pass? Perhaps "uncomprehended" is unfair; we cannot know, but it may be that while he was taking his hard long look at the desolate landscape Browning recognized a good deal of what he saw there. The evil Tower and the ambush of "hills, like giants at a hunting," spring up suddenly from the parched "dearth" of a waste land. Retrospectively the search through the waste for paths leading to the Dark Tower of abrupt menace amounts to a search for explanations. And as the Childe explores the ruined land he finds it strewn with symbolic stage properties and asks questions partially drawing out the implications of competitive struggle, factory miseries, and civil strife ruining a world. Browning, at least as the reader of his own poem, was unwilling and probably unable to draw them out fully. Contemporary readers did so chiefly in terms of "the struggle and aspiration of the soul." Since Browing did not apply labels like Tennyson's "jingling of the guinea" or "only the ledger lives" (while the poem which did name "gold" was published on a far distant page) they failed to see, or else they just took in stride, how large a component of his nightmare was industrial competition.

—David Erdman, "Browning's Industrial Nightmare," *Philological Quarterly* 36, no. 4 (1957): pp. 422, 427–29.

GEORGE M. RIDENOUR ON ALLEGORY IN "CHILDE ROLAND"

[George M. Ridenour has taught English at the University of New Mexico and the City University of New York. His publications include *The Style of Don Juan* (1960) and *Shelley: A Collection of Critical Essays* (1965). In this extract from the introduction to *Robert Browning: Selected Poetry* (1966), Ridenour examines "Childe Roland to the Dark Tower Came" as an example of Browning's "typical mode," one of four modes Ridenour coins in order to characterize Browning's various poetic attempts to unify his sense of reality.]

[T]he feeling grows that Browning's aim as a poet in the Romantic tradition is to devise forms in which the elements of reality as he experiences it may be contemplated as unified. (There seems to be at least a shift in emphasis in the development of Browning's poetry from problems of internal integration to those of perceiving reality itself as an integrated whole.) The list of attempted unions is imposing; power and love, love and knowledge, knowledge and power, imagination and reason, self and not-self, conscious and unconscious, spirit and matter, natural and supernatural, lyric and discursive, verse and prose. His attempts may usefully be broken down into at least four major types: the personal, the typical, the mythic, and the analytic. We may take "Fra Lippo Lippi" as representing the first, the vision of the dramatic monologues, where divisions are overcome in living, or which point toward harmony ironically through the dissonances of the speaker's life. The typical, mythic, and analytic modes, while not inherently more valuable, are in some ways harder to grasp, and it may be helpful to pay special attention to them. The modes will be examined by means of comment on poems drawn, like "Fra Lippo Lippi," from the great work of Browning's middle period, the *Men and Women* of 1855.

What I have called the typical mode may be seen most clearly in "Childe Roland to the Dark Tower Came." It is this typicality that causes our uneasiness in either calling the poem an allegory or in refraining from doing so. The knightly quest lends itself easily to allegorical treatment, because we are all of us looking for something all the time, in all our acts. The formality of the poem also encourages us to think of it as allegorical, even though it is not clear at once what it is allegorical of. This is especially striking since the allegorical mode invites simple and mechanical equation between the contents of the work and the world of values outside it. (This is true of even so refined a work as *The Faerie Queene*, as in the head-verses to the separate cantos. Though the poem is not limited to these crude equations, they influence our understanding of the dense and irreducible materials of the poem proper.) The allegory of "Childe Roland," in other words, is strangely self-contained, turning back on itself, so that the "allegoricalness" of the poem calls attention to itself as part of the meaning.

To shift the terms, allegory is apt to be strikingly rational and subrational, presenting a moral and conceptual organizing of the materials of fantasy; the moral will enters into close union with fierce unconscious drives. In Browning's poem the relations between the two elements are uncommonly problematic. This also tends to turn our attention into the poem in a manner unexpected in allegory, while we are still expecting the poem to fulfil its implied promise to be allegorical of something. One might be tempted to say, then, that the poem is an allegory of allegorizing (with Hawthorne's *Scarlet Letter* as partial analogy). But this would be too narrow, since the allegorical element is a metaphor of our attempts at directing our acts and at understanding them as purposive. It serves to represent the element of moral will in our acts and our understanding of those acts as directed by the moral will. It corresponds to our attempts, that is, at acting humanly for human goals—as "knights." The poem understood in this way becomes an allegory of what is involved in apparently purposeful human acts. It is "typical" of them.

> —George M. Ridenour, Introduction to *Robert Browning: Selected Poetry*, ed. George M. Ridenour (New York: The New American Library, 1966): pp. xi–xiii.

HAROLD BLOOM ON BROWNING'S RELATION TO SHELLEY

[In this extract from *The Ringers in the Tower* (1971), Harold Bloom sets Childe Roland's doomed quest against the background of the tradition of internalized romance, particularly as it is embodied in Shelley's poetry.]

To recognize Childe Roland as a Gnostic quester is to begin reading his poem as if it were a Borges parable of self-entrapment, another labyrinth made by men that men must decipher. A Gnostic quester is necessarily a kind of Quietist, for whom every landscape is infernal, and every shrine a squalor. In Shelleyan quest the objects of desire tend to touch the vanishing point of the visual and auditory, but the field of quest remains attractive, though not benign. Childe Roland moves in the Gnostic nightmare, where all natural context even looks and sounds malevolent, and the only goal of desire is to fail.

The greatest power of Browning's romance inheres not in its landscape (in which we are too ready to believe) but in the extraordinary, negative intensity of Childe Roland's consciousness, which brings to defeat an energy of perception so exuberant as to mock defeat's limits. This energy is very close to the remorseless drive of Shelley's Poet in *Alastor*, or of Shelley himself in *Epipsychidion*. The landscape of "Childe Roland to the Dark Tower Came," like that of *Alastor*, is charged by the quester's own furious, self-frustrated energy, and cannot at last contain that energy. When Childe Roland burns through the context he has invented, in his closing epiphany, he sees and hears all things he has made and marred, or rather made by breaking, himself and his vision, everything finally except the landscape of estrangement he has been seeing all through the poem. "Burningly it came on me all at once," he says, and "it" is place imagined into full meaning, an uncovering so complete as to be triumph whatever else comes to him. The Roland who sets the slug-horn to his lips does not accept a Gnostic conclusion, but ranges himself with those who have sounded the trumpet of a prophecy to unawakened earth. A poem that commenced in the spirit of *The Castle* or *Meditations In A Time of Civil War* concludes itself deliberately in the Orphic spirit of the *Ode To The West Wind*'s last stanza. ⟨. . .⟩

DeVane found much of the "source" material for Roland's landscape in Gerard de Lairesse's *The Art of Painting in All its Branches*, a book Browning remembered as having read "more often and with greater delight, when I was a child, than any other." Lairesse, celebrated by Browning in the late *Parleyings*, gathered together the horrible in painting, as he saw it, in his Chapter 17, *Of Things Deformed and Broken, Falsely called Painter-like*, and DeVane demonstrated how many details Browning took from the one chapter, probably unknowingly. Childe Roland, like Browning, is painter as well as poet, and dies as a living picture, framed by "all the lost adventurers my peers," who like him found all things deformed and broken.

All this is the living circumference of "Childe Roland to the Dark Tower Came"; we move to the central meaning when we ponder the sorrow of this quester, this *aware* solipsist whose self-recognition has ceased to be an avenue to freedom. When Roland ceased to imagine (before his poem opens) he made it inevitable that he should be *found by* his phantasmagoria. By marching into that land of his own terrible force of failed will, he compels himself to know the degradation of what it is to be illuminated while himself giving no light. For this is the anxiety of influence, in that variety of poetic melancholy that issues from the terrible strength of post-Enlightenment literary tradition. Where *Childe Roland* excels, and makes its greatness as a poem, is in its unique and appalling swerve, its twist or Lucretian *clinamen* away from its precursors, from the whole line of internalized romance, and from Shelley in particular. This swerve is the vision of the end, where *all* the poets of the Romantic tradition are seen as having failed, to the degree where they stand together, ranged in the living flame, the fire the Promethean quester could not steal but had to burn through.

Yet Childe Roland dies in the courage of knowing—he too sees, and he knows, and so dies with a full intelligence as what Keats called an atom of perception; at the close, he ceases to be a figure of romance, for he knows too much.

—Harold Bloom, *The Ringers in the Tower* (Chicago: University of Chicago Press, 1971): pp. 162–63, 165–66.

HAROLD BLOOM ON ROLAND'S FAILED QUEST

[In this extract from *A Map of Misreading* (1975), Harold Bloom reads "Childe Roland to the Dark Tower Came" in the context of his theory of poetic influence, locating at the poem's close a moment of judgment in which Roland critiques both his own failed quest and those of his poetic forebearers.]

Let me offer an explicit, indeed a reductive and therefore simplified total interpretation of the poem, firmly based on the model of misprision I have been tracing. There is no ogre at or in the Dark Tower for Roland to confront; the Tower is windowless and uninhabited, as blind as Roland's own fool's heart. "Fool" as a word goes back to the Latin *follis* for "bellows," and so a fool originally was a windbag. The root *bhel* means to blow or swell, which gives a triumphant twist to Roland's final act of blowing his slug-horn. In the *Song of Roland* this act is a signal to Roland's friends and is at the expense of almost the last breath of the mortally wounded hero. But Childe Roland's friends are disgraced and dead, and only the Childe's heart has been wounded, by the blind foolishness of questing for failure. Yet we feel, as readers, that death or at least mortal combat must be at hand as the poem ends. If Roland is alone at the end, as he is throughout the poem, then who is the antagonist? Certainly not "The Band" of brothers and precursors, for they stand ranged in vision, at the close. They may be a court in judgment, but they are there to see and to be seen, not to act.

There is only Roland himself to serve both as hero and as villain, only Roland to sound the trumpet as warning against Roland. The Childe stands in judgment against his own antithetical quest and, however lovingly, against his antithetical precursors as well. His blast on the slug-horn is an interpretation of his precursors' quest, which is to say that the poem becomes Browning's interpretation of a poem like Shelley's *Ode to the West Wind,* and perhaps of all Shelley's poetry. Roland sees himself at last as what he is, the solitary poet-quester, the *penseroso* so dangerously internalized as to have become anti-natural or antithetical, a counter-placing figure who stands against all the continuities that make life possible for the natural man. ⟨. . .⟩

As misprision, "Childe Roland to the Dark Tower Came" means the interplay of tropes, defenses, images that we have been studying. As *lidrosh,* interpretation, it means a de-idealizing critique of Shelley, but a wholly loving critique, one that exposes not the generous power of Shelley's trumpet of a prophecy, but something more of the experiential cost than the remorselessly noble Shelley would deign to acknowledge. As a Word of Browning's own brought forward, "Childe Roland" contrasts with Shelley's less psychologically revealing word, for Browning is a congeries of persons, and Shelley much more of a single being. Where the inspiration of Shelley is Orphic, Browning's is more unconditioned and absolute, because closer both to solipsism and to madness. The covenant between Shelley and Browning calls for a refusal to compromise with anything not in itself solitary and imaginative, and this covenant Browning has broken, with a consequent guilt present throughout Roland's monologue. But the Election-love burns on fiercely in Browning's Condition of Fire, as it will in Yeats's, for the sense of vocation in Roland as in Browning is renewed perpetually by Shelley's uncompromising and so both inspiring and chiding example. ⟨. . .⟩

The Childe's last act of dauntless courage is to will repetition, to accept his place in the company of the ruined. Roland tells us implicitly that the present is not so much negative and finite as it is willed, though this willing is never the work of an individual consciousness acting by itself. It is caught up in a subject-to-subject dialectic, in which the present moment is sacrificed, not to the energies of art, but to the near-solipsist's tragic victory over himself. Roland's negative moment is neither that of renunciation nor that of the loss of self in death or error. It is the negativity that is self-knowledge yielding its power to a doomed love of others, in the recognition that those others, like Shelley, had more grandly surrendered knowledge and its powers to love, however illusory. Or, most simply, Childe Roland dies, if he dies, in the magnificence of a belatedness that can accept itself as such. He ends in strength, because his vision has ceased to break and deform the world, and has begun to turn its dangerous strength upon its own defenses. Roland is the modern poet-as-hero, and his sustained courage to weather his own phantasmagoria and emerge into fire is a presage of the continued survival of strong poetry.

> —Harold Bloom, *A Map of Misreading* (Oxford: Oxford University Press, 1975): pp. 117, 119, 121–22.

ANNE WILLIAMS ON THE ARCHETYPAL CONTEXT OF "CHILDE ROLAND"

[Anne Williams teaches English literature at the University of Georgia and specializes in Romanticism and Feminist literary theory. Her books include *Prophetic Strain: The Greater Lyric in the Eighteenth Century* (1984) and *Art of Darkness: A Poetics of Gothic* (1995). Here Williams interprets Roland's quest as a revision of the archetypal hero's journey as outlined by Joseph Campbell in his *Hero With a Thousand Faces* (1949).]

The stages of Roland's experience, when compared with the composite picture of the traditional hero's quest (as outlined by, among others, Joseph Campbell in *The Hero With a Thousand Faces*) conform to a familiar and significant structure. Campbell summarizes the archetypal heroic quest in this way: "A hero ventures forth from the world of common day into a region of supernatural wonder: fabulous forces are there encountered and a decisive victory is won; the hero comes back from this mysterious adventure with the power to bestow boons on his fellow man." Since a "childe" is a young man preparing for knighthood, the suggestive pun on "child" as one innocent or inexperienced resonates with the conventional associations of the archetypal journey as a rite of initiation. But Browning's

Childe Roland is a long-tried and weary man, and he does not make the return journey. In its perfection, the heroic journey is circular; here we see only an arc, a portion of the journey toward the goal. And as Campbell writes, "If one or another of the basic elements of the archetypal pattern is omitted from a given fairy tale, legend, ritual, or myth, it is bound to be somehow or other implied—*and the omission itself can speak volumes for the history or pathology of the example*" (emphasis mine).

Campbell's names for the three stages the hero passes through are "Crossing the First Threshold," "The Belly of the Whale," and "The Road of Trials." The first seven stanzas describe Roland's entrance into the land of the unknown where adventure and discovery are possible. This entrance is watched by the conventional "threshold guardian." Like all such encounters, the meeting is seemingly random and accidental, and Childe Roland is understandably suspicious of the "hoary cripple" with "skull-like laugh" who, for the reader, suggests the traditional iconography of death as a skeleton. ⟨. . .⟩

The next stage, "The Belly of the Whale," is the part of the journey in which the hero is isolated, swallowed up by the unknown, "dead" to the world of external reality. After turning in the direction the cripple points, Childe Roland is immediately lost. ⟨. . .⟩

This isolation blends imperceptibly into the next stage, Campbell's "Road of Trials." Now the hero suffers in the strange land into which he has come. In "Childe Roland," the modifications—and thus the significance—of the quest pattern now become conspicuous. Roland is beset not by dragon, sorcerer, or temptress, but by his own fear, revulsion, loneliness, disgust, and hatred. His trials are psychological.

Yet two important stages of the monomyth have been omitted, both from the narrative and apparently from Roland's experience. Typically the hero's journey begins with "The Call to Adventure," when he leaves his everyday life to pursue the new goal. The last stage (and our knowledge) of Roland's search begins late, with the threshold guardian as he crosses into the wilderness; but we learn that although he has been seeking the Dark Tower all his life, he searches from no special devotion to a calling and perhaps not even from choice. ⟨. . .⟩

Childe Roland's solitude and isolation are as striking as his lack of wholehearted enthusiasm for the quest: he has no "Supernatural

Aid" (called for by Campbell's paradigm). Unlike other heroes, Childe Roland has not been given any magical talisman by a kind guardian, which (like King Arthur's Excalibur) supports the hero in time of need. Set upon the Road of Trials, Roland desires aid against despair. But he seeks it from within, in memories. ⟨. . .⟩

As Childe Roland reaches the Tower, the next stage of the monomyth is due to begin. Presumably arrival here at the goal of his "world-wide wandering" announces the presence of "The Ultimate Boon," revelation, and enlightenment. But here the last and most dramatic modification of this quest paradigm becomes evident. Because we know nothing of what happens at the Tower, our understanding of events is limited to the hero's before he becomes entirely a hero in the archetypal sense, before he knows more than we do. We follow him to the moment of revelation, but not into it. The poem pointedly gives only the finite human perspective on an experience of mysterious significance. ⟨. . .⟩

Childe Roland's quest is recognizable, then, as a variant of the monomyth outlined by Campbell, a fact which is useful in a number of ways. ⟨. . .⟩ In this context of heroic myth "Childe Roland" is clarified; and seeing so much that is suddenly familiar, we can be equally sensitive to what is not there: eager dedication to the quest, whatever it is, supernatural aid, and actual experience of the goal. This pattern supports the hypotheses that the journey is toward death. What universal human experience is more congruent with it? Man dies alone, unaided, and no living man can return to tell what lies on the other side.

—Anne Williams, "Browning's 'Childe Roland,' Apprentice for Night," *Victorian Poetry* 21, no. 1 (1983): pp. 28–29, 30, 31.

Thematic Analysis of
"Andrea del Sarto"

According to tradition, Browning wrote "Andrea del Sarto"—perhaps his single greatest monologue—as a response to his friend John Kenyon's request for a copy of Andrea del Sarto's self-portrait with his wife Lucrezia. Leery of copy costs in Florence, Browning sent his own "Andrea del Sarto" instead, and the poem can be viewed as an elaboration of the painting. Also in the background of the poem is Browning's debt to Giorgio Vasari's *Lives of the Artists,* which includes a sketch of Andrea's personal and artistic career. From Vasari Browning derived the idea of Andrea's reputation for technical perfection reflected in the poem's subtitle, "The Faultless Painter."

Though the poem's foremost focus is the issue of aesthetic failure, it begins with details surrounding a different kind of failure—the ruined romance between Andrea and Lucrezia. The poem represents a momentary suspension of the problems that characterize the relationship: its first line cuts a "quarrel" short and its last gives Lucrezia the go-ahead to meet her lover. Andrea asks Lucrezia to "bear with [him] for once," implying that her doing so would represent an exception to her normal habits. Significantly, Andrea predicates his ability to work—to paint—on Lucrezia's obliging his wish to sit hand-in-hand "by the window" with him "as married people use/Quietly, quietly the evening through."

This link between artistic inspiration and romance develops into one of the poem's primary themes. If Lucrezia had "but brought a mind" strong in proportion to her good looks, Andrea wistfully reasons, they "might have risen to Rafael" together. In Andrea's view, his own part in producing masterpieces is to supply the artistic skill; it is for Lucrezia to provide him with "soul" or passion. Toward the poem's conclusion Andrea suggests that the important difference between himself and the other great artists of Renaissance Italy is his marriage: "they overcome/Because there's still Lucrezia."

Yet for all Andrea's apparent interest in blaming Lucrezia for his shortcomings as an artist, he opposes to it a parallel explanation that rests on the idea of fate. Soon after he first makes the association between his career and his marriage, Andrea declares, "Love, we are in God's hand," which suggests that nothing could have changed what fate had in store for them. Bound by larger powers, Andrea is "fettered fast," and would accept the lot fate has accorded him rather than struggle vainly against it. By this view, it is neither Lucrezia's nor his own fault that Andrea has not reached greatness. But the speaker does not resolve the question by finally accepting any single account he considers. Instead, fate and failed romance coexist in a dialectic that continues throughout the poem, as Andrea tries to come to terms with the course his life has taken.

Amidst the uncertainties of figuring responsibility in the poem, the issue of Andrea's skill stands utterly resolved. Passing from romance and fate to the topic of his own reputation, Andrea allows himself a moment of righteous pride in what he has managed to achieve in spite of the handicaps of an unfaithful spouse and an unfavorable "lot" in life. Producing flawless paintings is, for Andrea, "easy," and he needs no "sketches first, no studies" to work from, but paints "perfectly" without preparation. But Andrea provides this account of his worth by way of acknowledging his limitations. "Well, less is more, Lucrezia," he states matter-of-factly, meaning that other artists' inferior technical endowments have not stood in the way of their grand ambitions.

Comparing himself to those artists that "reach many a time a heaven that's shut to me," Andrea indirectly reveals that his short-comings are in fact willed, that his failure is, to an extent, self-imposed. Ignoring his rivals and his wife alike, Andrea claims to paint "from [himself] and to [himself]." Rather than striving to transcend personal limitations, Andrea accepts them, thus assuring himself that he will experience neither the pain of artistic failure nor the glory of genuine artistic success. He declares that "a man's reach should exceed his grasp"—that the best artists push themselves beyond what they think they can do. Andrea, however, prefers not to engage in such agonizing pursuits: "All is silver grey/Placid and per-fect in my art: the worse!" In effect, Andrea trades the chance for greatness for the certainty of mediocrity, preferring the safety of low expectations to the risk of a rampant ambition.

That Andrea is not wholly without ambition, though, shows through his fond recollection of "that long festal year at Fountain-bleau," during which he enjoyed the patronage of King Francis I. By Vasari's account, Andrea's art flourished for the year he spent at

Fountainbleau, but his time there was cut short as he acquiesced to Lucrezia's demands to return to her in Florence. Andrea's nostalgic remembrance of his "kingly days" is riven with evidence of a need for an audience sympathetic to his work. Andrea paints "proudly with [Francis's] breath on" him, almost literally inspired by the attention. Too, Andrea credits Lucrezia for playing the part of his muse, "waiting on [his] work/To crown the issue with a last reward." For a moment, Andrea is tempted again to find in Lucrezia's infidelity—her having "grown restless"—reason for the diminution of his artistic aims. In keeping with Andrea's typically dialectical movement between fate and romance, Andrea soon ceases speculating on Lucrezia's role in determining his career to consider fate's part in shaping it. What emerges in spite of his constantly shifting rationales is a sense of his passivity, whether he seems dependent on the goodness of Lucrezia and Francis, or emphatically subject to the dictates of fate.

Whatever methods Andrea uses to "excuse" his underachieving mentality, his obsession with gauging his renown had he arduously applied himself becomes more and more clear. Much of the poem is located in the conditional past: what would have happened for him if things had been different? Having failed to join the likes of Rafael and Michelangelo in the uppermost echelon of Renaissance artists, Andrea nevertheless cherishes a grand notion of the eminence he could have achieved under different circumstances. By way of illustration, he relates an anecdote in which Michelangelo tells Rafael of Andrea's potential—how his abilities, applied with a proper dose of ambition, "would bring the sweat" onto Rafael's brow.

The poem's final hundred lines are fraught with the rhetoric of resolve, as Andrea repeatedly tries to come to grips with the partial fulfillment his career has brought him. Eager to persuade himself that life with Lucrezia is worth the sacrifice of his ambitions, Andrea "resolve[s] to think" that his fortunes have improved in the wake of leaving France for Florence. He strenuously reasons that the loss of "such a chance" for greatness will have been worthwhile if Lucrezia is herself "more pleased" with the situation as it stands. Testament to Andrea's interest in rationalizing his failure, he later contemplates the immutability of the past: "I regret little, I would change still less./Since there my past life lies, why alter it?" The dialectic underlying the poem thus provides Andrea with a pair of ways to stave off the pain of a lost opportunity. Both Lucrezia's ostensible happiness and the very fatality of the past help mitigate Andrea's sense of a greatness needlessly foregone.

The afterlife, for Andrea, represents the promise of compensation, and he ends his monologue by imagining a renewed opportunity to compete with "Leonard, Rafael [and] Agnolo" that will take place in heaven. The "four great walls" on which the contest will be staged belong to a string of tableau images in the poem that includes the "window" that affords the view of Fiesole, the "convent-wall" Andrea notes as he gazes at the city, and the "frame" his hands make as he clasps Lucrezia's face. The images center Andrea's optimism, and like the "four great walls" set forth toward the end of the poem, they represent an alternative past, one in which Andrea enjoys a sympathetic public, financial security, a faithful wife, and a place among the great artists of the time.

It is precisely the habit of shifting from images of life as it was to images of life as it might have been that most fully describes the logic of "Andrea del Sarto." To the very end Andrea remains perplexed by his past. Was it he who chose Lucrezia (as he says in the penultimate line of the poem) or fate that chose her for him? Could he have willed a triumph over circumstance or was his career always already out of his control? The poem represents a tremendously sophisticated portrait of a dialectical element in human psychology. Under the sway of his own dialectical temperment, various versions of the past vie and tangle with one another as Andrea tallies a lifetime of dubious gains and painful losses. ❈

Critical Views on
"Andrea del Sarto"

HENRY JAMES ON BROWNING'S PORTRAYAL OF
CHARACTER

[Henry James (1843–1916), a novelist and critic known for
his subtlety of perception and intricate style, wrote such
classics as *Daisy Miller* (1879), *The Portrait of a Lady* (1881),
and *Princess Casamassima* (1908). This extract is taken from
a brief essay written on the occasion of Browning's burial in
Westminster Abbey. James focuses on Browning's moder-
nity as well as his particular genius for capturing the finer
aspects of human character.]

It is as classics on one ground and another—some members of it
perhaps on that of not being anything less—that the numerous
assembly in the Abbey holds together, and it is as a tremendous and
incomparable modern that the author of *Men and Women* takes his
place in it. He introduces to his predecessors a kind of contemporary
individualism which surely for many a year they had not been
reminded of with any such force. The tradition of the poetic character as something high, detached and simple, which may be
assumed to have prevailed among them for a good while, is one that
Browning has broken at every turn; so that we can imagine his new
associates to stand about him, till they have got used to him, with
rather a sense of failing measures. A good many oddities and a good
man great writers have been entombed in the Abbey; but none of
the odd ones have been so great and none of the great ones so odd.
There are plenty of poets whose right to the title may be contested,
but there is no poetic head of equal power—crowned and recrowned
by almost importunate hands—from which so many people would
withhold the distinctive wreath. All this will give the marble phan-
toms at the base of the great pillars and the definite personalities of
the honorary slabs something to puzzle out until, by the quick oper-
ation of time, the mere fact of his lying there among the classified
and protected makes even Robert Browning lose a portion of the
bristling surface of his actuality.

For the rest, judging from the outside and with his contempo-
raries, we of the public can only feel that his very modernness—by

which we mean the all-touching, all-trying spirit of his work, permeated with accumulations and playing with knowledge—achieves a kind of conquest, or at least of extension, of the rigid pale. We cannot enter here upon any account either of that or of any other element of his genius, though surely no literary figure of our day seems to sit more unconsciously for the painter. The very imperfections of this original are fascinating, for they never present themselves as weaknesses; they are boldnesses and overgrowths, rich roughnesses and humours, and the patient critic need not despair of digging to the primary soil from which so many disparities and contradictions spring. ⟨. . .⟩

He was indeed a wonderful mixture of the universal and the alembicated. But he played with the curious and the special, they never submerged him, and it was a sign of his robustness that he could play to the end. His voice sounds loudest, and also clearest, for the things that, as a race, we like best—the fascination of faith, the acceptance of life, the respect for its mysteries, the endurance of its charges, the vitality of the will, the validity of character, the beauty of action, the seriousness, above all, of the great human passion. If Browning had spoken for us in no other way, he ought to have been made sure of, tamed and chained as a classic, on account of the extraordinary beauty of his treatment of the special relation between man and woman. It is a complete and splendid picture of the matter, which somehow places it at the same time in the region of conduct and responsibility. But when we talk of Robert Browning's speaking 'for us' we go to the end of our privilege, we say all. With a sense of security, perhaps even a certain complacency, we leave our sophisticated modern conscience, and perhaps even our heterogeneous modern vocabulary, in his charge among the illustrious.

> —Henry James, "Browning in Westminster Abbey," *The Speaker* (1890). Reprinted in *Robert Browning: A Collection of Critical Essays*, ed. Philip Drew (London: Methuen and Co., 1966): pp. 13–14, 15.

G. K. CHESTERTON ON BROWNING'S PHILOSOPHY

[Gilbert Keith Chesterton (1874–1936), a poet, novelist, critic, and journalist, wrote studies of many literary and religious figures, including Charles Dickens, Robert Louis Stevenson, and St. Thomas Aquinas. In this extract from *Robert Browning* (1926), which appeared in the highly regarded series ENGLISH MEN OF LETTERS, Chesterton discusses the two primary philosophical notions that run through Browning's poetry: the imperfection of the human and the imperfection of the divine.]

His two great theories of the universe may be expressed in two comparatively parallel phrases. The first was what may be called the hope which lies in the imperfection of man. The characteristic poem of "Old Pictures in Florence" expresses very quaintly and beautifully the idea that some hope may always be based on deficiency itself; in other words, that in so far as man is a one-legged or a one-eyed creature, there is something about his appearance which indicates that he should have another leg and another eye. The poem suggests admirably that such a sense of incompleteness may easily be a great advance upon a sense of completeness, that the part may easily and obviously be greater than the whole. And from this Browning draws, as he is fully justified in drawing, a definite hope for immortality and the larger scale of life. For nothing is more certain than that though this world is the only world that we have known, or of which we could even dream, the fact does remain that we have named it "a strange world." In other words, we have certainly felt that this world did not explain itself, that something in its complete and patent picture has been omitted. And Browning was right in saying that in a cosmos where incompleteness implies completeness, life implies immortality. This then was the first of the doctrines or opinions of Browning: the hope that lies in the imperfection of man. The second of the great Browning doctrines requires some audacity to express. It can only be properly stated as the hope that lies in the imperfection of God. That is to say, that Browning held that sorrow and self-denial, if they were the burdens of man, were also his privileges. He held that these stubborn sorrows and obscure valours might, to use a yet more strange expression, have provoked the envy of the Almighty. If man has self-sacrifice and God has none, then man has in the Universe a secret and blasphemous superiority. And this tremendous story of a Divine jealousy Browning reads into the story of the Crucifixion. If the Creator had not been crucified He would not have been as great as thousands of wretched fanatics among His own creatures. It is needless to insist upon this point; any one who wishes to read it splendidly expressed need only be referred to

"Saul." But these are emphatically the two main doctrines or opinions of Browning which I have ventured to characterise roughly as the hope in the imperfection of man, and more boldly as the hope in the imperfection of God. They are great thoughts, thoughts written by a great man, and they raise noble and beautiful doubts on behalf of faith which the human spirit will never answer or exhaust.

—G. K. Chesterton, *Robert Browning* (London: Macmillan and Co., 1926): pp. 177–79.

ROMA A. KING JR. ON LANGUAGE AND CHARACTER IN "ANDREA DEL SARTO"

[Roma A. King Jr. is Professor Emeritus at Ohio University, where he taught English literature. His works include *The Focusing Artifice: The Poetry of Robert Browning* (1968) and *Pattern in the Web: The Mythical Poetry of Charles Williams* (1990); he also edited an edition of Browning's *Complete Works* (1969). In this extract from *The Bow and the Lyre* (1957), King analyzes the way in which structural and linguistic aspects of "Andrea del Sarto" enhance the representation of character in the poem.]

The poem is a psychological study in which the time element is an important part of structure. Andrea's initial surrender to his wife's demand that he paint for money is totally damning to the artist; its completeness and finality divert interest from what may happen to why it has happened, from suspense in action to character analysis. The action moves from present to past, from past to present, and, finally, to an imaginary future in the New Jerusalem. Andrea's restless dissatisfaction with any time signals his personal disturbances, his unwillingness to accept himself in any role, real or imaginary, and provides a significant clue to the poem's meaning. ⟨...⟩

Diction, sound repetition, rhythm, and sentence structure all unite to create an impression, emotionally and sensuously, of placidity and greyness, qualities by which Andrea describes his life and work.

The diction, lacking the colorfulness of Fra Lippo Lippi's, is abstract and conceptual rather than perceptive and sensory. There are an unusually large number of substantives and relatively few modifiers, an almost equal number of concrete and abstract nouns. Clear and sharp but not particularly sensuous, the concrete nouns are used primarily to establish character and setting. Many are descriptive or technical: *sun, tree, star, moon, bird, picture, chalk.* Others show a painter's interest in man's anatomy: *hand, head, face, breast, ears, arms, neck, shoulders.* Andrea habitually speaks professionally, detachedly of the human body. It is as model that he refers most often to Lucrezia. ⟨. . .⟩

Alliteration is used further as part of rhythm. Stressing lightly conceptually unimportant syllables, and calling attention to others by heavy stress and alliteration, Browning achieves simultaneously in some lines both the artistic effect of alliterative verse and an emphasis on idea. Thus, the rhythmic pattern of the poem becomes a part of the meaning much more profoundly than by merely echoing the sense. Though irregular, the poem is "unmusical" only if judged by Spenserian and Tennysonian standards. Closer to the Wyatt-Donne tradition, Browning uses a line basically conventional in that it has a predetermined number of syllables and stresses, but breaks with the musical tradition in the placement of syllables within the line, proposing to relate closely what is felt and said with the manner of saying it, to use rhythm both to create and to support meaning. The absence of a strong sensuous movement, such as that, for example, which creates so vividly the physicality of Shakespeare's "Venus and Adonis" and Marlowe's "Hero and Leander," emphasizes Andrea's passivity; its brokenness reflects at the same time his psychological chaos. ⟨. . .⟩

The complex sentences, the numerous subordinations, the interpolations, the exclamations, the lack of syntactical connections give the effect of thought in conflict, of intellectual uncertainty and emotional instability. Andrea's aim is self-justification, but since he has not ordered his thinking, he cannot proceed straightforwardly as Lippo does; rather he muses disjointedly and inconclusively on first one aspect and then another of his unpleasant experience. Andrea is afraid to pursue his speculations to a logical conclusion for he partly knows and rejects what he would find if he did.

His sentences reflect the tortured flow of thought that can neither stop nor come to a logical conclusion, a surplus of diffused intensity that decreases the finality of what he says. The *pasticcio* quality of his thinking is demonstrated by the fact that a reader is hardly aware of either the beginning or the end of many of his constructions.

—Roma A. King Jr., *The Bow and the Lyre* (Ann Arbor: University of Michigan Press, 1957): pp. 11, 17, 19-20, 24.

HAROLD BLOOM ON THE ANXIETY OF REPRESENTATION

[In this extract from *Poetry and Repression: Revisionism from Blake to Stevens* (1976), Harold Bloom uses Nietzschean and Freudian insights to define the idea of belatedness as it is elaborated in the context of "Andrea del Sarto."]

Does Andrea overrate his own potential? If he does, *then there is no poem*, for unless his dubious gain-in-life has paid for a genuine loss-in-art, then he is too self-deceived to be interesting, even to himself. Browning has complicated this matter, as he complicates everything. The poem's subtitle reminds us that Andrea was called "The Faultless Painter," and Vasari, Browning's source, credits Andrea with everything in execution but then faults him for lacking ambition, for not attempting the Sublime. Andrea, in the poem, persuades us of a wasted greatness not so much by his boasting ("At any rate 'tis easy, all of it! / No sketches first, no studies, that's long past: / I do what many dream of, all their lives . . . "), but by his frightening skill in sketching his own twilight-piece, by his showing us how "A common greyness silvers everything—." Clearly, this speaker knows loss, and clearly he is the antithesis of his uncanny creator, whose poetry never suffers from a lack of ambition, who is always Sublime where he is most Grotesque, and always Grotesque when he storms the Sublime. Andrea does not represent anything in Browning directly, not even the betrayed relationship to the heroic precursor, yet he does represent one of Browning's anxieties, an anxiety related to but not identical with the anxiety of influence. It is an anxiety of representation, or a fear of forbidden meanings, or in Freudian language precisely a fear of the return-of-the-repressed, even though such a return would cancel out a poem-as-poem, or is it *because* such a return would end poetry as such?

Recall that Freud's notion of repression speaks of an unconsciously *purposeful* forgetting, and remind yourself also that what Browning could never bear was a sense of *purposelessness*. It is purposelessness that haunts Childe Roland, and we remember again what may be Nietzsche's most powerful insight, which closes the great Third Essay of *Towards the Genealogy of Morals*. The ascetic ideal, Nietzsche said, by which he meant also the aesthetic ideal, was the only *meaning* yet found for human suffering, and mankind would rather have the void *for* purpose than be void *of* purpose. Browning's great fear, purposelessness, was related to the single quality that had moved and impressed him most in Shelley: the remorseless purposefulness of the Poet in *Alastor*, of Prometheus, and of Shelley himself questing for death in *Adonais*. Andrea, as an artist, is the absolute antithesis of the absolute idealist Shelley, and so Andrea is a representation of profound Browningesque anxiety. ⟨. . .⟩

We enter again the dubious area of *belatedness*, which Browning is reluctant to represent, but is too strong and authentic a poet to avoid. Though Andrea uses another vocabulary, a defensively evasive one, to express his relationship to Michelangelo, Raphael, and Leonardo, he suffers the burden of the latecomer. His Lucrezia is the emblem of his belatedness, his planned excuse for his failure in strength, which he accurately diagnoses as a failure in will.

—Harold Bloom, *Poetry and Repression: Revisionism from Blake to Stevens* (New Haven: Yale University Press, 1976): pp. 192–93.

HERBERT F. TUCKER ON THE IMPERFECT IN "ANDREA DEL SARTO"

[Herbert F. Tucker's analysis of "Andrea del Sarto" focuses on the way in which Andrea appropriates the notion of the imperfect in order to evade the struggles that come with ambition.]

In the background of Andrea's accommodating autobiographical scheme lies his version of the Browningesque philosophy of the imperfect: "Ah, but a man's reach should exceed his grasp, / Or what's a heaven for?" That these lines, along with Pippa's "God's in his heaven" (from *Pippa Passes*), should have been untimely ripped from context and delivered up as Browning's moral of life is not quite the irony of literary history that it would appear; or, if there be irony, it is Browning's and is already written into his poetry. It is remarkable that Browning should have entrusted his cherished beliefs to so devious a speaker as Andrea. Betty Miller steps with convincing ease from poetry to biography and finds the poem a confession of Browning's besetting psychosexual weaknesses. Yet the very proximity of Andrea to Browning, and the remarkable extent of Browning's dramatic trust in writing this monologue, may also be taken as indexes of poetic strength. "Andrea del Sarto" represents one of Browning's most intimate engagements with a threat he greatly feared: the tendency of poetic meaning generally, and of his own deep-running convictions in particular, to precipitate a doctrine—or, in Andrea's phrase, "to fall into a shape." ⟨. . .⟩

Once teaching has hardened into doctrine, it becomes a commodity that a technician as clever as Andrea can use for his own ends. Andrea has taught himself enough of the doctrine of imperfection to insure that he need never undergo the growing pains of further learning. He sees formal failings in the works of Rafael and of lesser painters in Florence and sees too that these failings testify to a grandeur withheld. Andrea determines to aggrandize himself by multiplying the advantage of his doctrinal lever and outfailing them all. ⟨. . .⟩

Where others discover a frustrating gap between reach and grasp, between their excessive aspirations and the limits of their technical capabilities, Andrea frustrates himself in advance by arranging an equal and opposite gap between grasp and reach. Literally self-effacing at line 197 ("Ay, but the soul! he's Rafael! rub it out!"), Andrea purposely intends less than he can perform so that he may number himself among the "half-men," the glorious failures of art, without enduring their struggles. His doctrine of imperfection shows him the low road into a compensatory heaven, one that he ultimately prefers to the heaven of artists who "Reach many a time a heaven that's shut to me" and of Rafael, "Reaching, that heaven might so replenish him, / Above and through his art." In the celestial vision of the New Jerusalem that ends the poem, Andrea reaffirms this preference, "choosing" to be "overcome" by more aspiring artists, the better to repay himself with an afterlife providing renewed opportunity and support for a lifelong habit of regret. Such is the power of Andrea's calculated impotence that it will transform "four great walls in the New Jerusalem" into a cozier place where he will feel more at home: "The grange whose four walls make his world." ⟨...⟩

"How could it end in any other way?" Andrea's question is an instance of the rhetoric of self-fulfilling divination that recurs throughout the monologue. "So free we seem, so fettered fast we are!"; "All is as God over-rules"; "God is just"; "Let each one bear his lot"; "No doubt, there's something strikes a balance." Delighted that character is fate, Andrea sings in his fetters a hymn celebrating the divinely poetic justice, the pleasing aesthetic balance, of the life he has freely contrived for himself. The entire monologue falls into shape as a faultlessly rounded episode in this life. Andrea bargains for his hour with Lucrezia in the full expectation that he will lose her to her lover; the opening promise that "all shall happen as you wish" also foretells that all shall happen as Andrea wishes. By preempting the pain of his loss from the beginning, he becomes the knowing author of its fated inevitability and comes into the commanding strength of his final, imperative "Go, my Love."

—Herbert F. Tucker Jr., *Browning's Beginnings: The Art of Disclosure* (Minneapolis: University of Minnesota Press, 1980): pp. 196, 197–98, 200.

Thematic Analysis of
"Caliban Upon Setebos"

Perhaps the most critically acclaimed of the poems in *Dramatis Personae* (1864), "Caliban Upon Setebos" reflects the intellectual furor that arrived in the wake of the 1859 publication of Darwin's *The Origin of Species*. The principle of evolution that Darwin elaborates is central to the poem, but "Caliban" also needs to be read against other backgrounds, including the "natural theology" of William Paley (1743–1805) and the doctrine of predestination of orthodox Calvinism. In *Natural Theology* (1802) Paley argued that the world of nature affords evidence of God's designs and intelligence. Calvinism taught that while humans possess free will, they are at the same time predestined in accordance with God's purposes. The speaker's prototype is the Caliban of Shakespeare's late romance *The Tempest*, who embodies the bestial, not having been "honor'd with a human shape." A significant part of the poem's importance derives from its position at a nexus of Victorian culture, whether its relation to its origins—Darwin, Paley, Calvin, and Shakespeare—be considered satiric or sympathetic.

The brackets enclosing the poem's first section mark it as a kind of unspoken prelude to the rest of the poem. The poem's first phrase demonstrates Caliban's habit of referring to himself in the third-person: it is Caliban himself who "'Will sprawl, now that the heat of day is best.'" This strange tendency emphasizes Caliban's interest in hiding from Setebos, as if declaring his presence through a first-person pronoun would render his self-concealment ineffective. Caliban retreats into a cave by the sea in order to "talk to his own self" about Setebos freely, without fear of drawing an angry reaction.

Having situated himself safely, Caliban sets about speculating on Setebos, attempting to piece together an account of the deity based on experiential evidence. At the heart of his speculation lies an empiricist ethic, the limitations of which are in large part responsible for the portrait of Setebos that emerges. Because Caliban's reasoning and imagination are limited by what he has experienced, the Setebos he develops ends up looking a lot like Caliban. The phrase "so He," repeated throughout the poem, encapsulates this logic of resemblance. He suggests, for example, that Setebos's creation of the world "came of being ill at ease": as James Loucks notes, the idea that Setebos is uneasy is a direct projection of Caliban's own misery. Similarly, to rationalize what he experiences as divine ambivalence, Caliban refers to his own observation of "an icy fish" who is drawn to and then repulsed by a warmer realm of the sea. Unable to relocate, the fish returns to the cold water she came from, "hating and loving warmth alike," just as Setebos seems to both hate and love out of a kind of frustration.

Creation, by Caliban's account, proceeds as a direct result of Setebos's mixed feelings, and he catalogues like a naturalist might the creatures that inhabit the world around him to support this idea. "Spite" is Setebos's primary impetus. Not completely satisfied, unable to make "a second self/To be His mate," and unlikely to create beings "he mislikes or slights," the god chooses to produce lesser versions of himself—"things He admires and mocks too." Setebos, Caliban reasons, makes beings "worthy" of his own interest, and occasionally ones that are "better" than him, but their bravery and other strengths never threaten their maker: "It nothing skills if He begin to plague."

Himself a fanciful individual, Caliban imagines a fanciful Setebos who glories in arbitrary displays of power. To come to terms with the god's approach to earthly intervention, Caliban works from a hypothesis in which he creates "a live bird out of clay." Just as Setebos seems to ignore the sufferings of his creatures, so Caliban imagines he would "laugh" if his newly created bird "lay stupid-like" with a "snapped" leg. Answering the bird's prayers Caliban likewise relegates to a matter of mood: "this might take or else/Not take my fancy." The more Caliban compares himself to Setebos, the more sympathetic to the deity's situation he seems to become. The seemingly random pattern of divine intervention suggests neither kindness nor cruelty in the creator, but rather indifference.

Midway through the monologue, Caliban returns to the question of the origins of divine disgruntlement: "But wherefore rough, why cold and ill at ease?/Ah that is a question!" As the brute's own unhappiness derives from the presence of a capricious creator, Caliban posits a similarly inscrutable deity above Setebos. Under the thumb of the "Quiet," Setebos leads an unsatisfactory existence that he relieves, at least to some degree, by making a "bauble-world to ape" the real one. Anticipating Freud's notion of mastery through repetition, Caliban remarks that there is solace in "making baubles": creating a substitute world of one's own allows for a gratifying illusion of control. He then confesses to turning this wisdom into practice himself, having captured a "four-legged serpent" he pretends is Miranda, a "tall pouch-bill crane" to be his Ariel, and even a "sea-beast" to represent himself, as he plays and thus consoles himself "with make-believes."

The "weakness" both Caliban and the creatures around him exhibit results from Setebos's interest in "sport." In possession of more or less all of his wants, Setebos has occasions neither to love nor hate: that he created the world must mean, according to Caliban, that Setebos simply likes to work for "work's sole sake." In such a world without purpose, creatures' imperfections can only be signs of a divine predilection for drama or "sport." Caliban likens Setebos's personality to his own during the easy-going and safe "summer-time." Just as Setebos created and may destroy the world on a whim, so Caliban constructs an equally unuseful "pile of turfs" he might "some day knock . . . down" just to enjoy the pleasure of power.

In Caliban's view, there is no possibility of living in accordance with Setebos's will, which operates on a central premise of unpredictability. The deity Caliban envisions is essentially a proud one, a god who "may grow wroth" if "you . . . play him off" with a too-assured understanding of "His ways." Caliban accounts for the unpredictability by comparing himself to Setebos: what would irk him most would be a similar affectation of knowledge in a creature below him. Power, for Caliban, inheres precisely in its arbitrary usage; the animal below him that guesses his mind steals something of his strength.

The poem ends with a return to the inward speech the brackets indicate. A storm begins, and as Caliban cowers before it, he notices the departure of a raven he worries will inform Setebos of his heretical musings. Having come to a fuller understanding of Setebos's ways, Caliban assumes a humble posture and promises to forego food so long as he may esscape retribution. In spite of his hope that "the Quiet" might "catch/And conquer Setebos," thus establishing a new, perhaps more just dispensation, Caliban comes full circle, resuming a stance of slavish misery.

"Caliban Upon Setebos" frames questions about the origins and motives of the divine. Regardless of its possibly satirical tone, the monologue takes up philosophical and religious conundrums that run all through cultural history. Like many of Browning's best poems, it cherishes no single resolution but rather dramatizes a moment in a process that acquires moral, psychological, social, and spiritual inflections as it is fleshed out. Like "Childe Roland to the Dark Tower Came," "Caliban" features an in-depth exploration of the act of interpretation itself, and both poems can ultimately be seen to stage an heroic but nonetheless doomed quest for a correct reading of nature. ❁

Critical Views on
"Caliban Upon Setebos"

WALTER BAGEHOT ON THE GROTESQUE

[Walter Bagehot (1826–1877), an economist and journalist, published widely on politics, banking, and literature and edited *The National Review.* In this extract from an essay on Wordsworth, Tennyson, and Browning, Bagehot defines and examines the presence of the grotesque in Browning's work, particularly as it inheres in "Caliban Upon Setebos."]

Grotesque [art] shows you what ought to be by what ought not to be, when complete it reminds you of the perfect image, by showing you the distorted and imperfect image. Of this art we possess in the present generation one prolific master. Mr. Browning is an artist working by incongruity. Possibly hardly one of his most considerable efforts can be found which is not great because of its odd mixture. He puts together things which no one else would have put together, and produces on our minds a result which no one else would have produced, or tried to produce. ⟨. . .⟩

Mr. Browning has undertaken to describe what may be called *mind in difficulties*—mind set to make out the universe under the worst and hardest circumstances. He takes 'Caliban,' not perhaps exactly Shakespeare's Caliban, but an analogous and worse creature; a strong thinking power, but a nasty creature—a gross animal, uncontrolled and unelevated by any feeling of religion or duty. The delineation of him will show that Mr. Browning does not wish to take undue advantage of his readers by choice of nice subjects. ⟨. . .⟩

A thinking faculty more in difficulties—a great type,—an inquisitive, searching intellect under more disagreeable conditions, with worse helps, more likely to find falsehood, less likely to find truth, can scarcely be imagined. Nor is the mere description of the thought at all bad: on the contrary, if we closely examine it, it is very clever. Hardly anyone could have amassed so many ideas at once nasty and suitable. But scarcely any readers—any casual readers—who are not of the sect of Mr. Browning's admirers will be able to examine it enough to appreciate it. From a defect, partly of subject, and partly of style, many of Mr. Browning's works make a demand upon the reader's zeal and sense of duty to which the nature of most readers is unequal. They have on the turf the convenient expression 'staying power': some horses can hold on and others cannot. But hardly any reader not of special and peculiar nature can hold on through such composition. There is not enough of 'staying power' in human nature.

We are not judging Mr. Browning simply from a hasty recent production. All poets are liable to misconceptions, and if such a piece as 'Caliban Upon Setebos' were an isolated error, a venial and particular exception, we should have given it no prominence. We have put it forward because it just elucidates both our subject and the characteristics of Mr. Browning. . . .

Mr. Browning possibly, and some of the worst of Mr. Browning's admirers certainly, will say that these grotesque objects exist in real life, and therefore they ought to be, at least may be, described in art. But though pleasure is not the end of poetry, pleasing is a condition of poetry. An exceptional monstrosity of horrid ugliness cannot be made pleasing, except it be made to suggest—to recall—the perfection, the beauty, from which it is a deviation. Perhaps in extreme cases no art is equal to this; but then such self-imposed problems should not be worked by the artist; these out-of-the-way and detestible subjects should be let alone by him. It is rather characteristic of Mr. Browning to neglect this rule. He is the most of a realist, and the least of an idealist of any poet we know.

—Walter Bagehot, "Wordsworth, Tennyson, and Browning; or Pure, Ornate, and Grotesque Art in English Poetry," *The National Review* 19 (November 1864). Reprinted in *Browning: The Critical Heritage*, ed. Boyd Litzinger and Donald Smalley (London: Routledge and Kegan Paul, 1970): pp. 274–76.

George Santayana on Browning's Temperament

[George Santayana (1863–1952) was a philosopher and poet who made important contributions to aesthetics and literary criticism. His works include *The Sense of Beauty* (1896), *The Life of Reason* (1905–06), and *Realms of Being*

(1928) among others. In this extract from "The Poetry of Barbarism," Santayana discusses the absence in Browning's work of any strict metaphysics, finding a correlation between what he perceives as the "barbarism" of Browning's temperament and the obsession with the immediate that his work exemplifies.]

The nineteenth century, as we have already said, has nourished the hope of abolishing the past as a force while it studies it as an object; and Browning, with his fondness for a historical stage setting and for the gossip of history, rebelled equally against the Pagan and the Christian discipline. The 'Soul' which he trusted in was the barbarous soul, the 'Spontaneous Me' of his half-brother Whitman. It was a restless personal impulse, conscious of obscure depths within itself which it fancied to be infinite, and of a certain vague sympathy with wind and cloud and with the universal mutation. It was the soul that might have animated Attila and Alaric when they came down into Italy, a soul not incurious of the tawdriness and corruption of the strange civilization it beheld, but incapable of understanding its original spirit; a soul maintaining in the presence of that noble, unappreciated ruin all its own lordliness and energy, and all its native vulgarity. ⟨. . .⟩

Browning's philosophy of life and habit of imagination do not require the support of any metaphysical theory. His temperament is perfectly self-sufficient and primary; what doctrines he has are suggested by it and are too loose to give it more than a hesitant expression; they are quite powerless to give it any justification which it might lack on its face.

It is the temperament, then, that speaks; we may brush aside as unsubstantial, and even as distorting, the web of arguments and theories which it has spun out of itself. And what does the temperament say? That life is an adventure, not a discipline; that the exercise of energy is the absolute good, irrespective of motives or of consequences. These are the maxims of a frank barbarism; nothing could express better the lust of life, the dogged unwillingness to learn from experience, the contempt for rationality, the carelessness about perfection, the admiration for mere force, in which barbarism always betrays itself. The vague religion which seeks to justify this attitude is really only another outburst of the same irrational impulse.

In Browning this religion takes the name of Christianity, and identifies itself with one or two Christian ideas arbitrarily selected; but at heart it has far more affinity to the worship of Thor or of Odin than to the religion of the Cross. The zest of life becomes a cosmic emotion; we lump the whole together and cry, 'Hurrah for the Universe!' A faith which is thus a pure matter of lustiness and inebriation rises and falls, attracts or repels, with the ebb and flow of the mood from which it springs. It is invincible because unseizable; it is as safe from refutation as it is rebellious to embodiment. ⟨. . .⟩

Such barbarism of temper and thought could hardly, in a man of Browning's independence and spontaneity, be without its counterpart in his art. When a man's personal religion is passive, as Shakespeare's seems to have been, and is adopted without question or particular interest from the society around him, we may not observe any analogy between it and the free creations of that man's mind. Not so when the religion is created afresh by the private imagination; it is then merely one among many personal works of art, and will naturally bear a family likeness to the others. The same individual temperament, with its limitations and its bias, will appear in the art which has appeared in the religion. And such is the case with Browning. His limitations as a poet are the counterpart of his limitations as a moralist and theologian; only in the poet they are not so regrettable. Philosophy and religion are nothing if not ultimate; it is their business to deal with general principles and final aims. Now it is in the conception of things fundamental and ultimate that Browning is weak; he is strong in the conception of things immediate. The pulse of the emotion, the bobbing up of the thought, the streaming of the reverie—these he can note down with picturesque force or imagine with admirable fecundity.

—George Santayana, *Interpretations of Poetry and Religion* (New York: Scribners, 1900): pp. 24, 29, 30.

CONSTANCE W. HASSETT ON THE SUSPENSION OF IDENTITY IN "CALIBAN UPON SETEBOS"

[Constance W. Hassett teaches English literature at Fordham University and is the author of *The Elusive Self in the Poetry of Robert Browning* (1982), from which this extract is taken. Here Hassett discusses a crucial dynamic in "Caliban Upon Setebos": how the subjective aspect of perception comes to color and limit understanding.]

The self-concern that leads Andrea to misconstrue his past causes some of Browning's characters to misinterpret external reality. In "Caliban upon Setebos," he shows how the needs that distort confession affect an individual's cosmogony as well. Andrea's and Caliban's motives are basically the same, only their methods differ. The limitations the one refuses to acknowledge, the other ascribes to his god. Projection replaces evasion as a delusive strategy, and Setebos is actually Caliban's own self, admired and feared as a deified other.

More powerful and content than Caliban, Setebos is, nonetheless, cold, ill at ease, and far from absolute. He exists in mysterious subordination to the Quiet and his inferiority fascinates Caliban. Assuming that Setebos is dissatisfied with his state but unable to "soar / To what is quiet and hath happy life," Caliban supposes that the god expresses his envy by making a "bauble-world to ape yon real." This world-crafting activity is little more than spiritually impoverished play, a solace for his own insufficiency.

What interests Browning about these speculations is the way Caliban's personality limits his perception. Incapable of any more positive emotion than generalized spite, he cannot conceive of a generous motive for the act of creation. His view of the originating principle, as critics have noted, is outrageously at odds with the traditional notion of generative fecundity. The dialogist of the "Timaeus" and generations of Christian Platonists who follow suppose that "he who did construct [the universe] was good, and in one that is good, no envy of anything ever arises. Being devoid of envy then he desired that everything should be so far as possible like himself." The principle of goodness, in other words, requires that everything should have being. ⟨. . .⟩

Neither Caliban nor his god, however, is moved by any such goodness or fullness. Creation, in Caliban's view, is not the bringing into existence of every possible good; on the contrary, Setebos "made all these and more, / Made all we see, and us, in spite: how else?" The god is thought to be inspired by the inaccessibly worthier reality of the Quiet world and, for the sake of a spurious kind of transcendence, to fashion an imitation world that is deliberately and service-ably diminished. ⟨. . .⟩

At the bottom of Caliban's theory is his own inability to establish a truly creative relationship with Prospero's world. He cannot imaginatively locate himself there. Incapable of self-transcendence and genuine expansion of consciousness, he produces only mutilated versions of the reality he cannot penetrate. In a deftly ironic bit of drama Browning allows Caliban to improvise his own counterpart. Compelled by his discontent, he blinds a "lumpish" sea creature, pens it in a hole and calls it by his own name. This charade of self-mastery is wholly inconsequential, however, and leaves Caliban as unenlightened as ever about himself or the beast. But the episode suggests a distinction that is important for Browning's art. A subjective aesthetic leaves one ignorant, whereas true creation, because it requires the suspension of one's habitual identity, is a means of discovery. When the personality of the maker is allowed to dominate, then the created object, whether an artifact or a verbal construct, a world or a worldview, is only a deceitful alternative to reality. This is the paradox of Browning's own practice in the dramatic monologue. True art—and in this sense the most deeply personal—must be impersonal.

—Constance W. Hassett, *The Elusive Self in the Poetry of Robert Browning* (Athens, Ohio: Ohio University Press, 1982): pp. 96, 97.

STEVEN SHAVIRO ON CALIBAN'S INTERPRETIVE DILEMMA

[Steven Shaviro teaches English literature at the University of Washington and is the author of *Passion and Excess* (1990) and *The Cinematic Body* (1993). In this extract, Shaviro focuses on Caliban's obsessively repetitive and ultimately doomed struggles to develop an account of himself through questing after his own origins.]

Caliban himself may be most satisfactorily characterised as the obsessive interpreter *par excellence.* He reads nature as a text with a hidden author, and ceaselessly endeavors to fix within an elaborate interpretative scheme himself and everything he encounters. The major trope of "Caliban Upon Setebos" is the argument from design of natural theology. But reading the book of nature is no easy task for this mid-nineteenth-century savage theologian. Nature, on this island, is violent, unstable, and chaotic; Caliban is incessantly compelled to make new adjustments to his theories, and to put forth ever new analogies, in order to keep up with the unceasing flow of new ideas, facts, and experiences. He argues from a design which is constantly threatening to dissolve. Shakespeare's Caliban seemed to possess a fixed position upon the Great Chain of Being; whereas Browning's monster lives within an anarchy of competing forces.

It is in response to this impossibility of interpretation, this unlimited phenomenality, that theology becomes a teleology, that essence is defined solely in terms of origin. Caliban strives to reduce chaos by discovering a hidden order and cause, and to account for his own being, and that of the universe around him, by determining what creative activity was the origin of himself and of his world. The trope of evolution first generates the figure of Caliban as primitive man, and is then adopted as Caliban's own method of reasoning. Browning returns us to the origins of theology, only to present us with a theology of origins. Such a transposition is inherent in any genetic interpretation: when essence is located in origin, origin itself becomes part of that unending process which is all that is left of essence, and is thereby subverted. There is an origin or ancestral point at the start of human existence, from which all of mankind has evolved; yet this origin is itself only a (missing) link, a mediator between ourselves and something even more ancient. Even (or especially) as a primitive man or representative of human origins, Caliban is already caught up in a process which exceeds and precedes him, as it is beyond his own control. ⟨...⟩

Caliban's first act of interpretation—motivated from his position as victim—is to postulate Setebos as the origin and cause of whatever discomforts and anxieties he suffers. The interpretative drive for mastery is thus itself only a product of the negative, deprived, reactive state of misery and lack. Caliban's first act of natural theologizing does not free him from the greater purposelessness of being trapped as a passive victim of what he regards as Setebos's inscrutable designs. A more active response becomes necessary. Mastery is achieved, after a fashion. But such mastery is itself still tied, in obsessive repetition, to the condition of deprivation and lack which motivates it.

—Steven Shaviro, "Browning Upon Caliban Upon Setebos," *Browning Society Notes* 12, nos. 2–3 (1983): pp. 3–4, 16.

J. HILLIS MILLER ON BROWNING'S METAPHYSICS

[J. Hillis Miller has taught literature at Williams College, Johns Hopkins University, and Yale University. Currently on the faculty of the University of California at Irvine, Miller's many works include *Charles Dickens* (1958), *Poets of Reality* (1965), *The Linguistic Moment* (1985), *Victorian Subjects* (1990), and *Topographies* (1995). In this extract, Miller documents the presence of the transcendental in Browning's oeuvre, locating a sense of optimism in Browning's aesthetic of the imperfect.]

This failure of romantic Prometheanism causes Browning to make a radical transformation in his poetry. After *Sordello*, instead of writing poetry which is disguised autobiography, the autobiography of Prometheus in search of the divine fire, Browning writes dramatic monologues, that is, as he said, "poetry always dramatic in principle, and so many utterances of so many imaginary persons, not mine." The dramatic monologue presupposes a double awareness on the part of its author, an awareness which is the very essence of historicism. On the one hand the dramatic monologuist is aware of the relativity of any single life or way of looking at the world. He sees each one from the outside as merely one possible life, and yields himself with a certain irony or detachment to one after another of these imagined selves. But on the other hand the monologuist is also aware that reality, for us human beings, lies only in a life which is immersed in a material and social world, and living with all its energy the life appropriate to that situation. The only sin is the refusal to act or make choices, for "a crime will do / As well . . . to serve for a test, / As a virtue golden through and through," and man must above all avoid "the unlit lamp and the ungirt loin." Reality for man is the inexhaustible multiplicity of all the lives which have ever been lived or could be lived, and it is these which the modern poet, the poet of historicism, must describe.

So we get the great gallery of idiosyncratic individuals in Browning's most famous poems: scoundrels, quacks, hypocrites, cowards, casuists, heroes, adulterers, artists, Bishop Blougram, Mr Sludge the Medium, the Bishop ordering his tomb. The reality of each of these lives lies in its limitation, its narrowness. It is one special way of living in the world chosen out of all the infinite possibilities. Browning seems to have committed himself wholeheartedly, like Nietzsche or Gide, to a life of perspectivism or role-playing. ⟨. . .⟩

The philosophical and aesthetic moral of *The Ring and the Book* is: "By multiplying points of view you may transcend point of view, and reach at last God's own infinite perspective." Slowly, bit by bit, the different versions of the story, like the distancing of the facts in the depths of the historical past, liberate the poem from being a "false show of things," and make of the eccentric interpretations an elaborate oblique incantation which evokes the truth, that divine truth at the center of each finite person or event which, in Browning's view, can never be faced directly or said directly. ⟨. . .⟩

But this way of dealing with the absence of God ultimately fails. Even though we may agree that each finite human perspective is an authentic version of the world, even though we may agree that it contains one spark of the divine plenitude, nevertheless, however many of these fragmentary glimpses of God we may add up, we shall be no closer to the whole, or to a face to face confrontation with God. ⟨. . .⟩

It turns out, however, that in this failure lies unsuspected success. For man's perpetual striving is his most God-like attribute. Only if Browning closes himself off is he finished for good, and excluded forever from God. As long as he keeps moving he is in God's grace, and imitates in little the very life of God. The uncouth, half-finished statues of Michelangelo are more in correspondence to the deity than any smooth perfection, and the form of Browning's poetry, in its internal contradictions, its rough-hewn quality, its openendedness, is the very image of infinity, and of the limitless perfection of God. God himself constantly transcends himself, and moves into ever-new spheres of being. On earth we are in a sense already in heaven, for in heaven we shall exist in the same dynamic motion as on earth, continually going beyond ourselves even as here. Though God is not temporal, the driving motion of time is a perfect image of his explosive eternity.

—J. Hillis Miller, *Victorian Subjects* (London: Harvester Wheatsheaf, 1990): pp. 57–58, 59–60.

Works by
Robert Browning

Pauline. 1833.

Paracelsus. 1835

Strafford. 1837.

Sordello. 1840.

Bells and Pomegranates. 1841–46.

Dramatic Lyrics. 1842.

Dramatic Romances and Lyrics. 1845.

Christmas Eve and Easter Day. 1850.

Men and Women. 1855.

Dramatis Personae. 1864.

The Ring and the Book. 1868–9.

Balaustion's Adventure. 1871.

Prince Hohenstiel-Schwangau. 1871.

Fifine at the Fair. 1872.

Red Cotton Night Cap Country. 1873.

Aristophanes' Apology. 1875.

The Inn Album. 1875.

Pacchiarotto and How He Worked in Distemper: With Other Poems. 1876.

The Agamemnon of Aeschylus. 1877.

La Saisiaz and the Two Poets of Croisic. 1878.

Dramatic Idyls (First Series). 1879.

Dramatic Idyls (Second Series). 1880.

Jocoseria. 1883.

Ferishtah's Fantasies. 1884.

Parleyings with Certain People of Importance in Their Day. 1887.

Asolando: Fancies and Facts. 1889.

Works about
Robert Browning

Altick, Richard Daniel. *Browning's Roman Murder Story: A Reading of 'The Ring and the Book.'* Chicago: University of Chicago Press, 1968.

Armstrong, Isobel. *Victorian Poetry: Poetry, Poetics and Politics.* London: Routledge, 1993.

———, ed. *Writers and Their Background: Robert Browning.* Athens: Ohio University Press, 1975.

Bloom, Harold, ed. *Robert Browning.* New York: Chelsea House, 1985.

Bloom, Harold, and Adrienne Munich, eds. *Robert Browning: A Collection of Critical Essays.* Englewood Cliffs, N.J.: Prentice Hall, 1979.

Chesterton, G. K. *Robert Browning.* London: Macmillan, 1903.

Cook, Eleanor. *Browning's Lyrics: An Exploration.* Toronto: University of Toronto Press, 1974.

Crowell, Norton B. *The Convex Glass: The Mind of Robert Browning.* Albuquerque: University of New Mexico Press, 1968.

De Vane, William Clyde, and Kenneth Leslie Knickerbocker, eds. *New Letters.* New Haven: Yale University Press, 1950.

De Vane, William Clyde. *A Browning Handbook.* New York: F. S. Crofts and Co., 1935.

Drew, Philip. *The Poetry of Robert Browning: A Critical Introduction.* London: Methuen, 1970.

Duckworth, Francis F. G. *Browning: Background and Conflict.* Hamden, Conn.: Archon Books, 1966.

Erdman, David. "Browning's Industrial Nightmare." *Philological Quarterly* 36, no. 4 (1957): 417–35.

Erickson, Lee. *Robert Browning: His Poetry and Audiences.* Ithaca: Cornell University Press, 1984.

Flowers, Betty S. *Browning and the Modern Tradition.* London: Macmillan, 1976.

Gridley, Roy E. *Browning.* London: Routledge and Kegan Paul, 1972.

Griffin, William Hall. *The Life of Robert Browning.* Hamden, Conn.: Archon Books, 1966.

Harrold, William. *The Variance and the Unity: A Study of the Complementary Poems of Robert Browning.* Athens: Ohio University Press, 1973.

Hassett, Constance W. *The Elusive Self in the Poetry of Robert Browning.* Athens: Ohio University Press, 1982.

Honan, Park. *Browning's Characters: A Study of Poetic Technique.* Hamden, Conn.: Archon Books, 1969.

Irvine, William. *The Book, the Ring and the Poet.* New York: McGraw Hill, 1974.

Jack, Ian. *Browning's Major Poetry.* Oxford: Clarendon Press, 1973.

Jack, Ian, and Margaret Smith, eds. *The Poetical Works of Robert Browning.* New York: Oxford University Press, 1983.

Johnson, Edward D. H. *The Alien Vision of Victorian Poetry: Sources of the Poetic Imagination in Tennyson, Browning and Arnold.* Hamden, Conn.: Archon Books, 1963.

King, Roma A., Jr., *The Bow and the Lyre: The Art of Robert Browning.* Ann Arbor: University of Michigan Press, 1957.

———. *The Focusing Artifice: The Poetry of Robert Browning.* Athens: Ohio University Press, 1968.

———, et al., eds. *The Complete Works of Robert Browning.* Athens: Ohio University Press, 1969.

Kintner, Elvan, ed. *The Letters of Robert Browning and Elizabeth Barrett Browning, 1845–1846.* Cambridge, Mass.: Belknap Press, 1969.

Litzinger, Boyd. *The Browning Critics.* Lexington: University of Kentucky Press, 1965.

Litzinger, Boyd, and Donald Smalley, eds. *Browning: The Critical Heritage.* London: Routledge and Kegan Paul, 1970.

Loucks, James F., ed. *Robert Browning's Poetry.* New York: W. W. Norton and Co., 1979.

Maynard, John. *Browning's Youth.* Cambridge: Harvard University Press, 1977.

Miller, Betty Bergson. *Robert Browning: A Portrait.* New York: Scribners, 1953.

Pottle, Frederick. *Shelley and Browning: A Myth and Some Facts.* Chicago: Pembroke Press, 1923.

Ricks, Christopher, ed. *The Brownings, Letters and Poetry*. Garden City, N.Y.: Doubleday, 1970.

Ridenour, George M., ed. *Robert Browning: Selected Poetry*. New York: New American Library, 1966.

Ryals, Clyde de. *Becoming Browning: The Poems and Plays of Robert Browning*, 1833–1846. Columbus: Ohio State University Press, 1983.

———. *Browning's Later Poetry, 1871–1889*. Ithaca: Cornell University Press, 1975.

Shaviro, Steven. "Browning Upon 'Caliban Upon Setebo.'" *Browning Society Notes* 12, nos. 2–3 (1983): 3–18.

Shaw, William David. *The Dialectical Temper: The Rhetorical Art of Robert Browning*. Ithaca, N.Y.: Cornell University Press, 1968.

Starzyk, Lawrence J. "Browning and the Ekphrastic Encounter." *Studies in English Literature, 1500–1900* 38, no. 4 (1998): 689–706.

Sussman, Herbert. "Robert Browning's 'Fra Lippo Lippi' and the Problematic of a Male Poetic." *Victorian Studies* 35, no. 2 (Winter 1992): 185–200.

Thomas, Donald. *Robert Browning: A Life Within Life*. London: Weidenfield and Nicholson, 1982.

Tucker, Herbert F. *Browning's Beginnings: The Art of Disclosure*. Minneapolis: University of Minnesota Press, 1980.

Wagner-Lawlor, Jennifer A. "The Pragmatics of Silence, and the Figuration of the Reader in Browning's Dramatic Monologues." *Victorian Poetry* 35, no. 3 (1997): 287–302.

Williams, Anne. "Browning's 'Childe Roland,' Apprentice for Night." *Victorian Poetry* 21, no. 1 (Spring 1983): 27–42.

Index of
Themes and Ideas